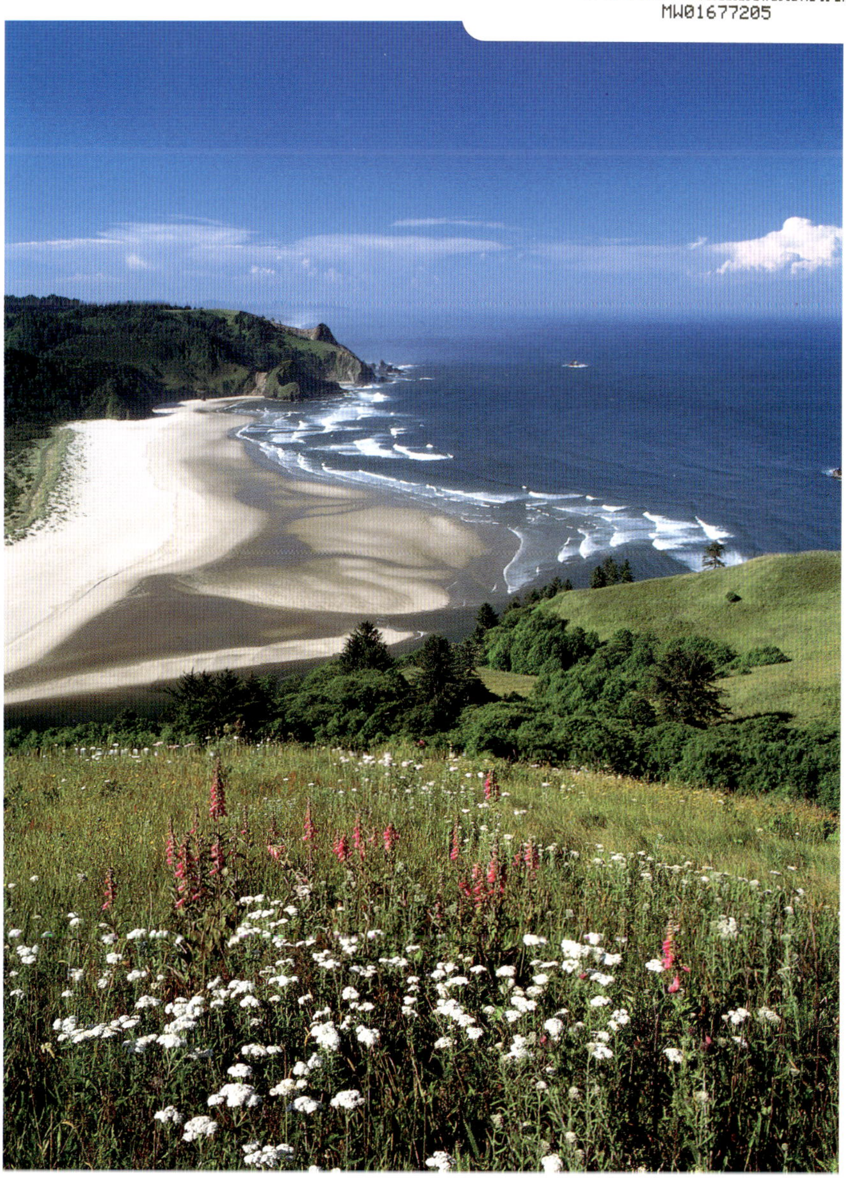

Flowered headland and Salmon River Estuary at Cascade Head
(Central Coast) LARRY GEDDIS

Uplifted underwater lava flows spawned the 1,200 foot-high headland and nearby islands where seabirds crowd steep cliffs, and bald eagles and hawks can be spotted soaring above the grassy slopes.

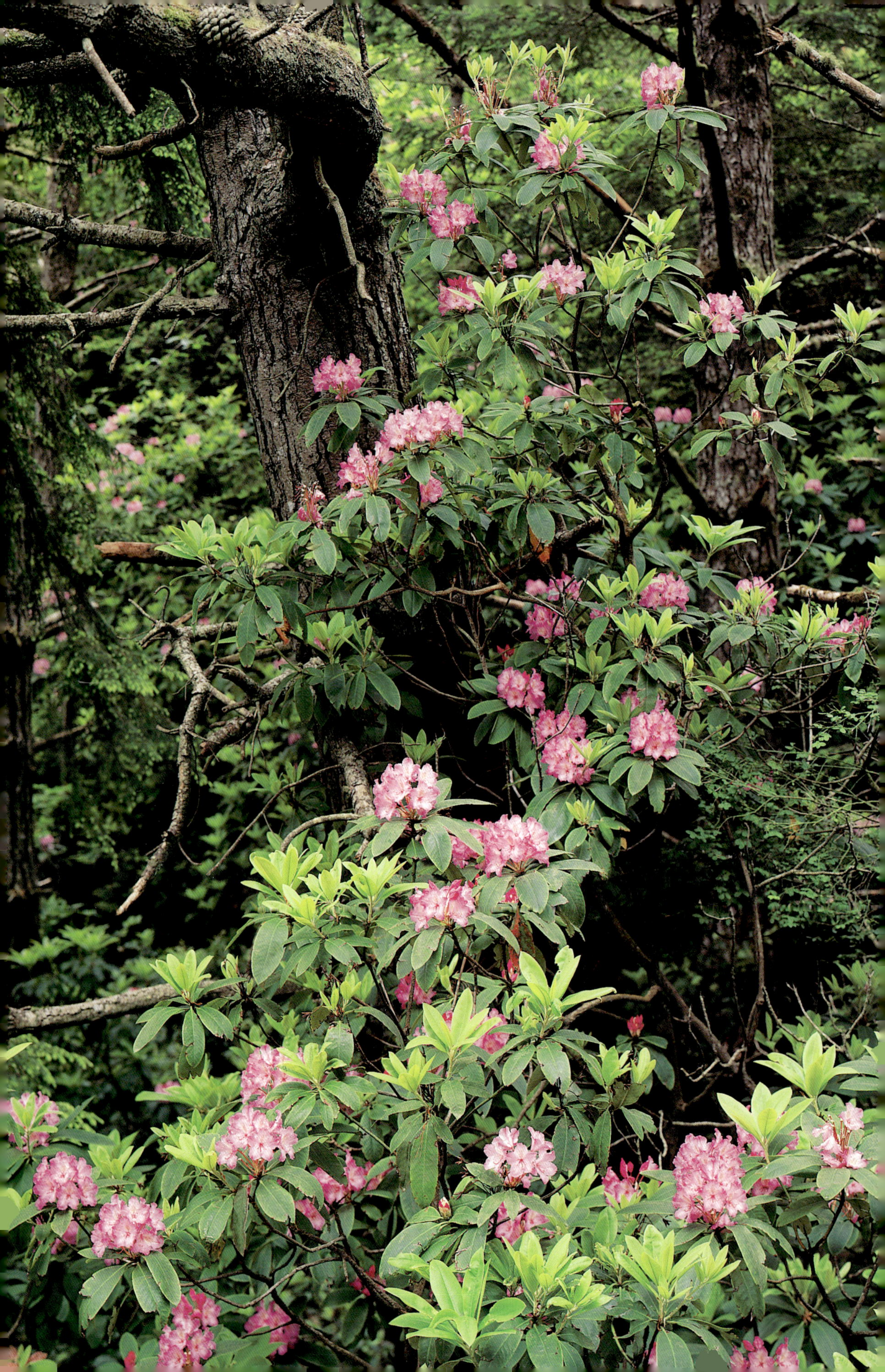

Arts of Earth
OREGON COAST
impressions

Photography by

LARRY GEDDIS

STEVE TERRILL

CHARLES & ANNE JACOBS

Text by

LARRY GEDDIS

Published by Arts of Earth
P.O. Box 19324
Portland, Oregon 97280

Front Cover:
From Ecola State Park, clouds pass over Haystack Rock and Cannon Beach
(Northern Coast) CHARLES JACOBS

Back Cover:
A giant wave meets the sandstone cliffs at Shore Acres State Park
(Southern Coast) LARRY GEDDIS

Opposite Title Page:
Coastal rhododendrons bloom among a grove of rare Monterey pine trees in Oregon Dunes National Recreation Area
(Central Coast) STEVE TERRILL

International Standard Book Number: 0-9655963-0-3

Printed in Hong Kong

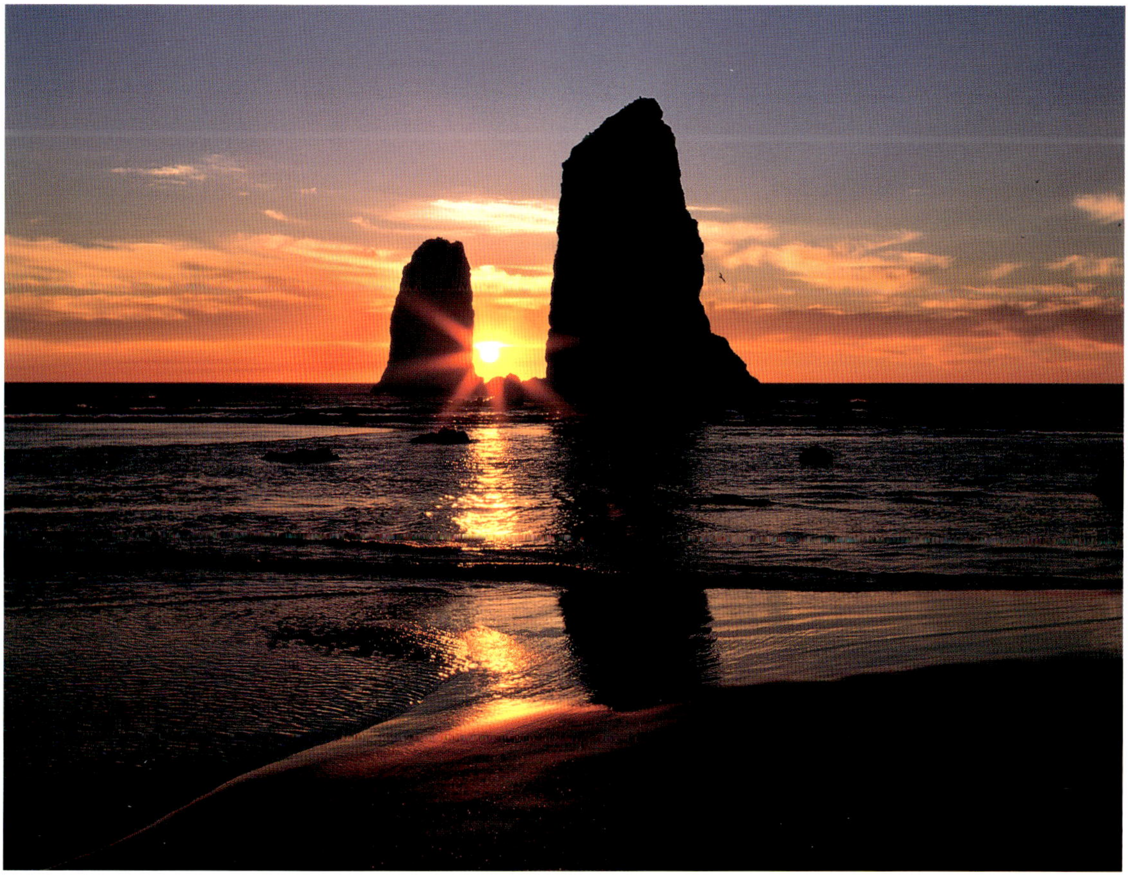

Sunset silhouettes the "Needles" at Cannon Beach *(Northern Coast)* LARRY GEDDIS

September 10, 1846, the U.S.S. Shark, on a mission to make depth soundings, wrecked on the Columbia River bar. The ship broke up and drifted close to this spot. The cannon and a large part of the deck washed ashore; hence the name, Cannon Beach.

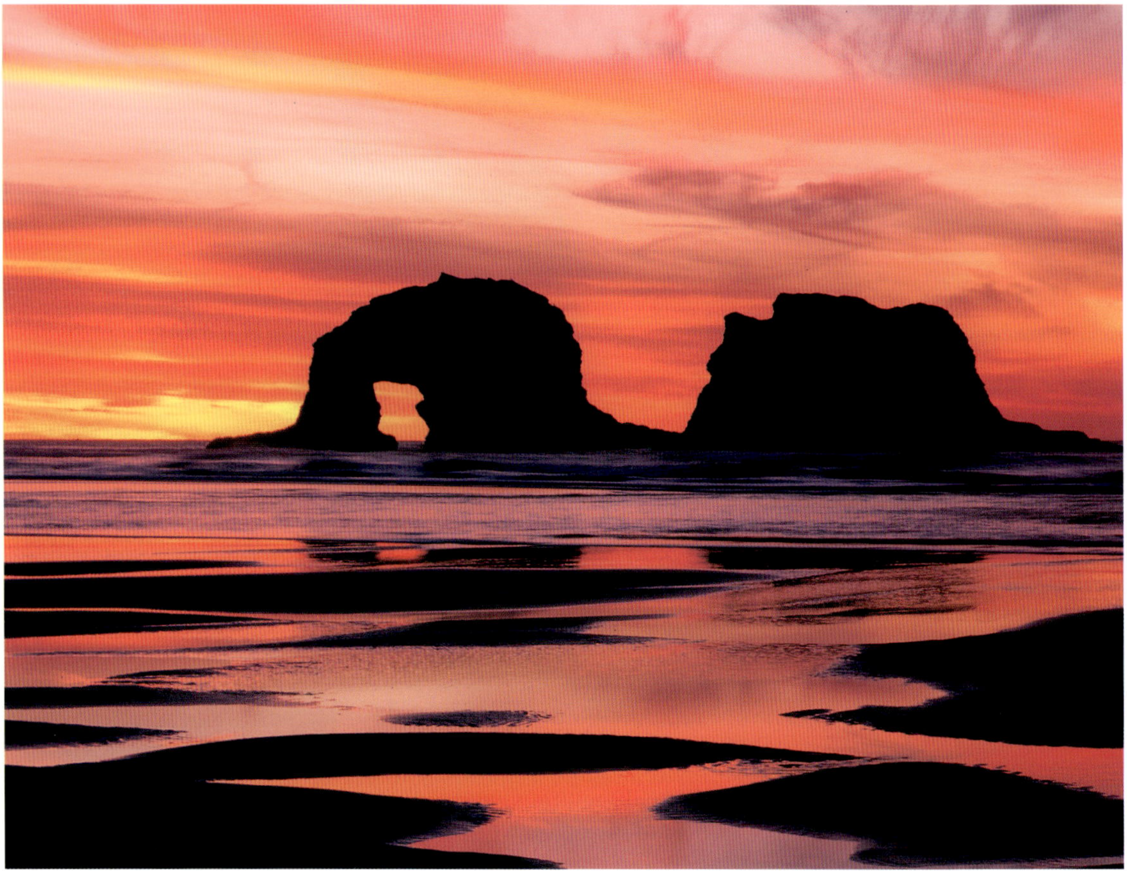

Spectacular sunset silhouettes Twin Rocks at Rockaway *(Northern Coast)* Larry Geddis

The Oregon Coast

From Astoria in the north, to Brookings in the south, the Oregon coast covers 362 miles in length.

In my opinion, no other coastline in the world can match the beauty found along the Oregon coast. Magnificent headlands, rocky coves, sandy beaches, offshore sea stacks, and beautiful vistas are found all along the way.

After seventeen years of living in Oregon, my wife and I still can not be pressed into stating which area of the Oregon coast is our favorite. Who can choose which is the best spot along the Oregon coast? Is it on the northern coastline with a view from Ecola State Park on a foggy morning? Is it the smell of salt air from Cascade Head on the central coastline? Or is it the sound of a crashing wave at Shore Acres State Park on the southern coastline?

For this reason, the photographs that appear in this book showcase the unique geographic diversity of Oregon's northern, central, and southern coastline.

The photographs selected for this book represent the natural beauty of our coast. Other than a lighthouse, a kite, or a fishing boat, no photographs showing man-made objects were considered. It is my heartfelt wish that the photography in this book will inspire all of us to preserve and protect the pristine beauty of the Oregon coast for future generations to enjoy. The coast of Oregon is not only a state treasure, but also a national treasure to be protected at all costs.

Larry Geddis

Following Pages:
Autumn sunrise over Cannon Beach from Ecola State Park
(Northern Coast) Steve Terrill

Captain William Clark of the Lewis and Clark Expedition wrote in his 1806 journal of this viewpoint, "...the grandest and most pleasing prospects which my eyes ever surveyed."

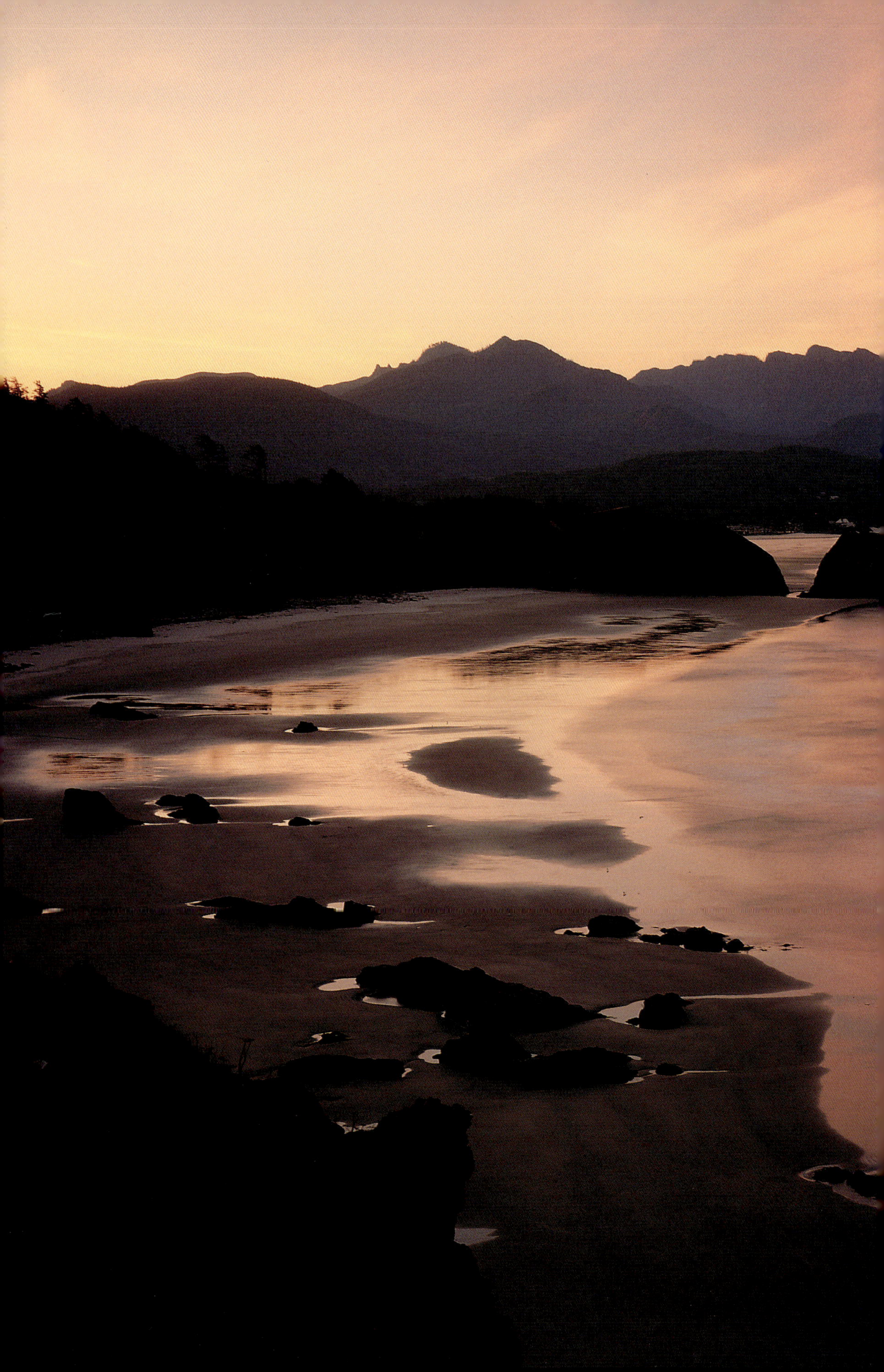

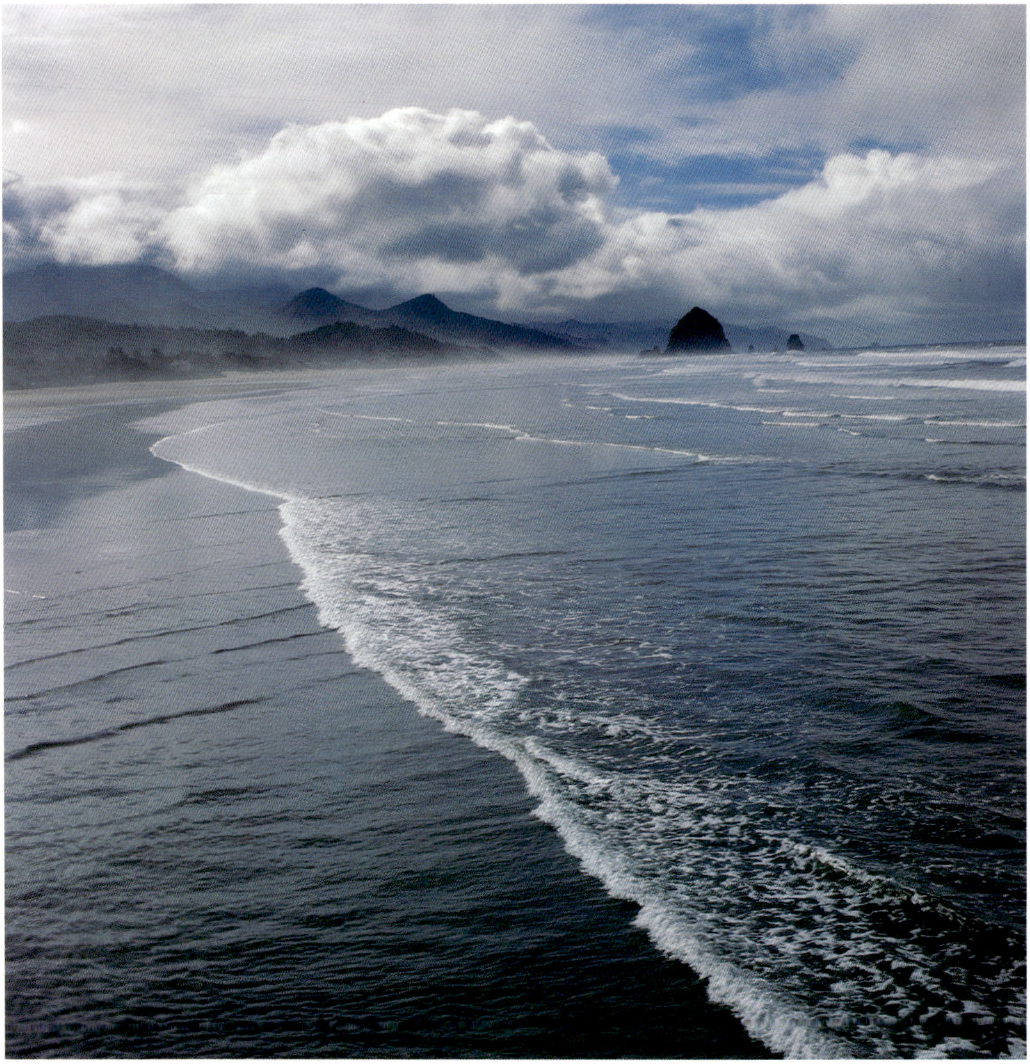

Clouds and surf meet at Cannon Beach with Haystack Rock
(Northern Coast) Charles Jacobs

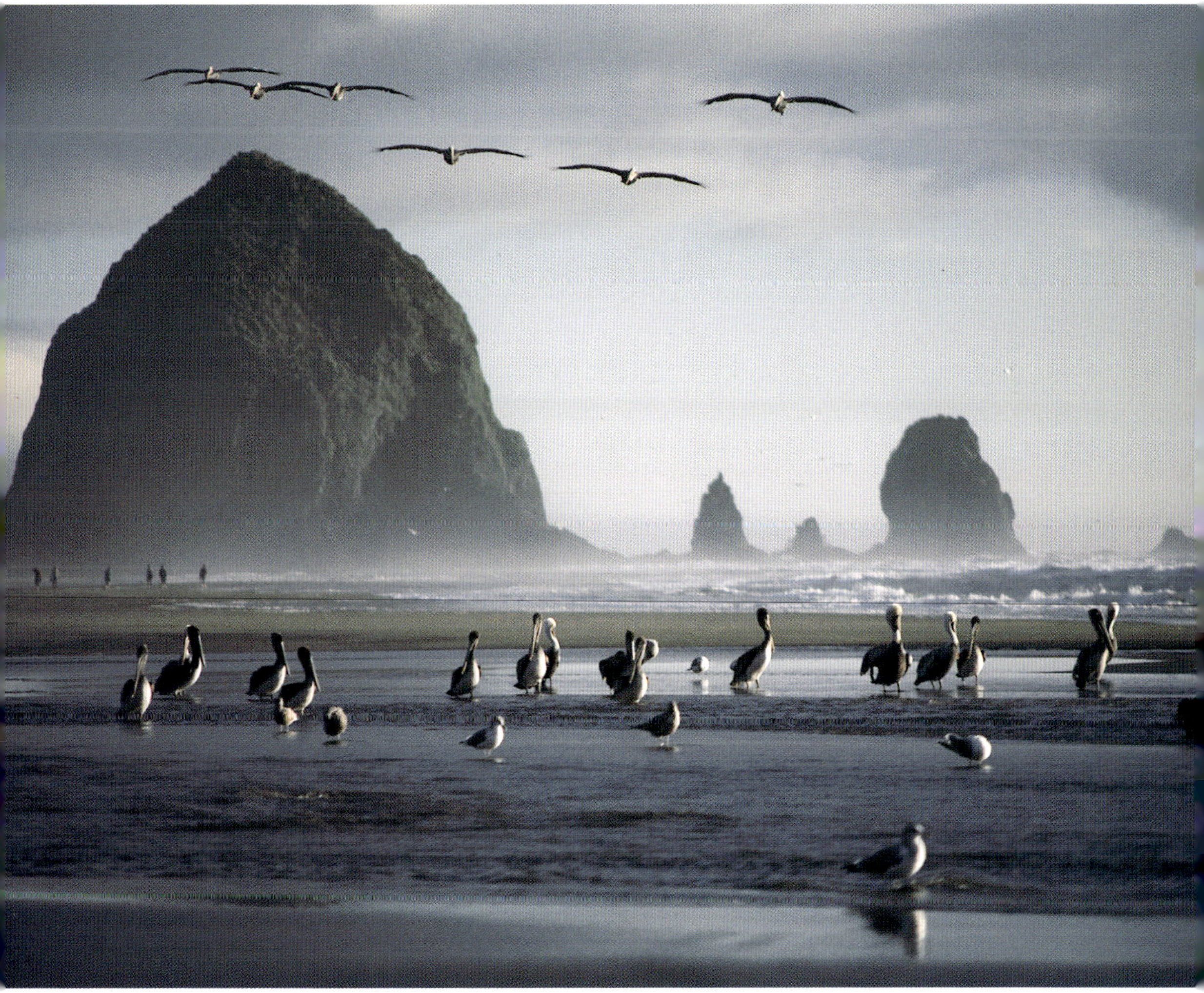

Pelicans soar over Haystack Rock for a landing on Cannon Beach *(Northern Coast)* Anne Jacobs

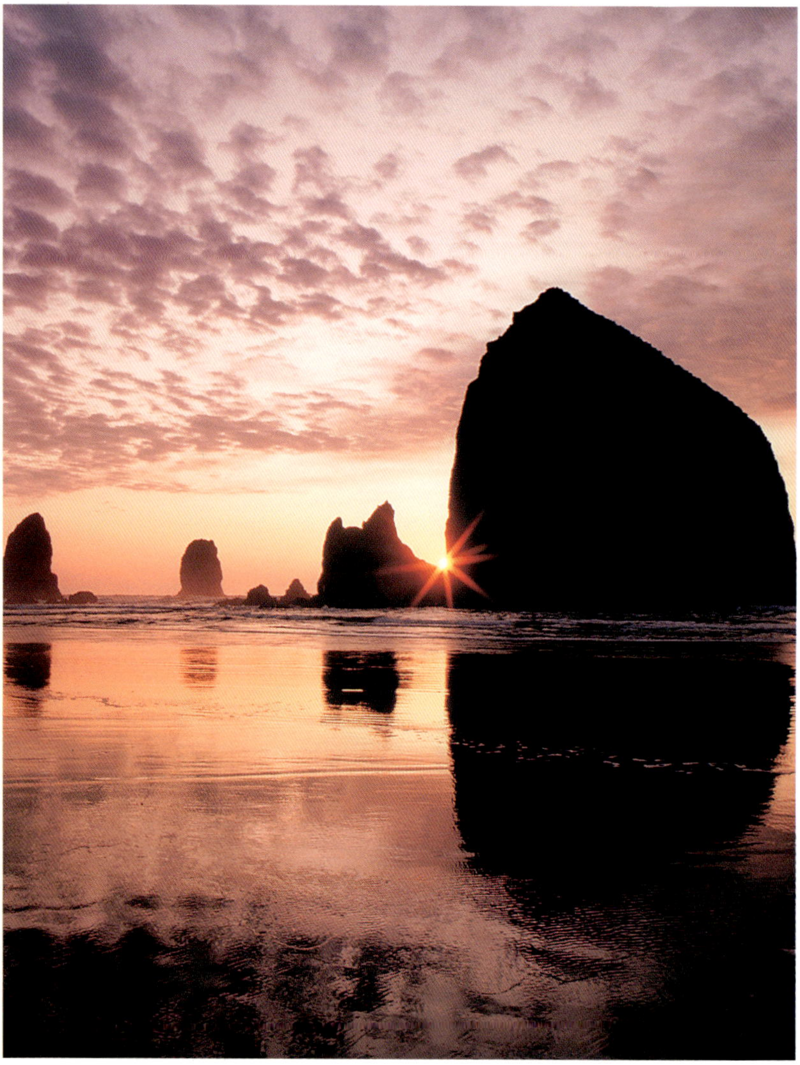

Sunset at Haystack Rock, Cannon Beach
(Northern Coast) LARRY GEDDIS

Rising 235 feet, Haystack Rock is one of the largest monoliths in the world.

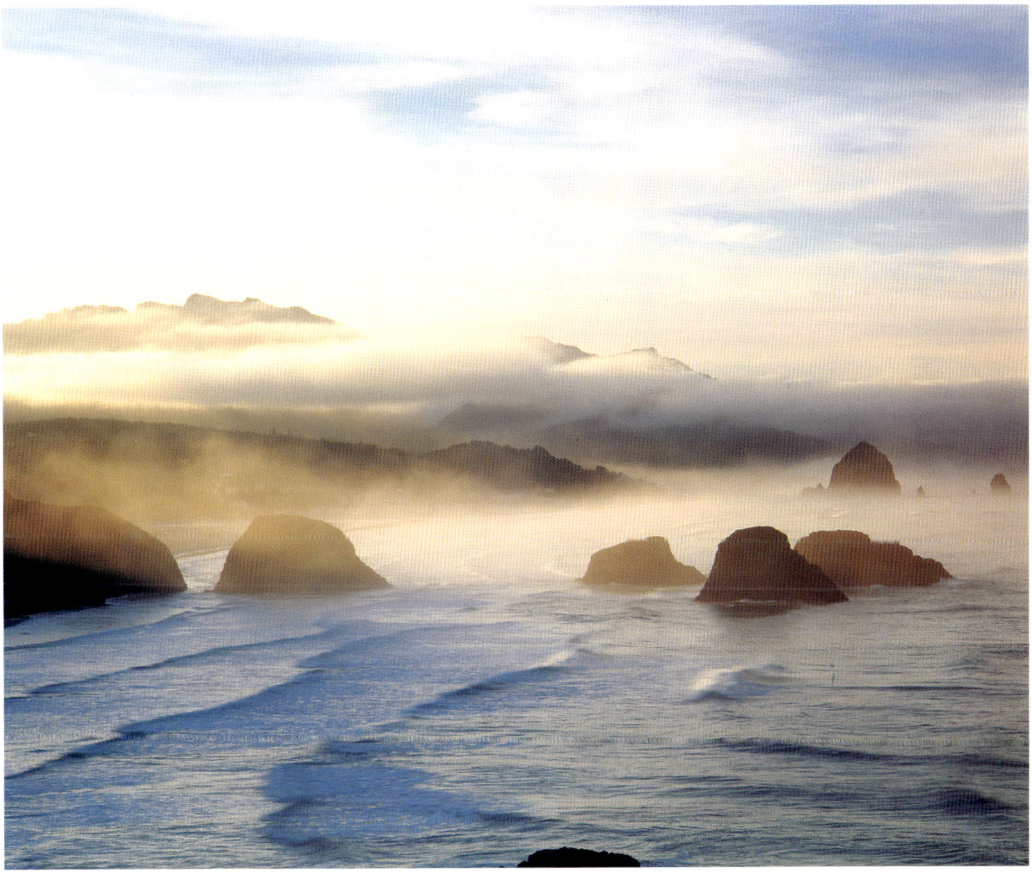

From Ecola State Park, early morning fog settles over Cannon Beach
(Northern Coast) STEVE TERRILL

Ecola is the Clatsop Native American word for "whale," which inspired members of the Lewis and Clark expedition to name this area after seeing a whale washed ashore.

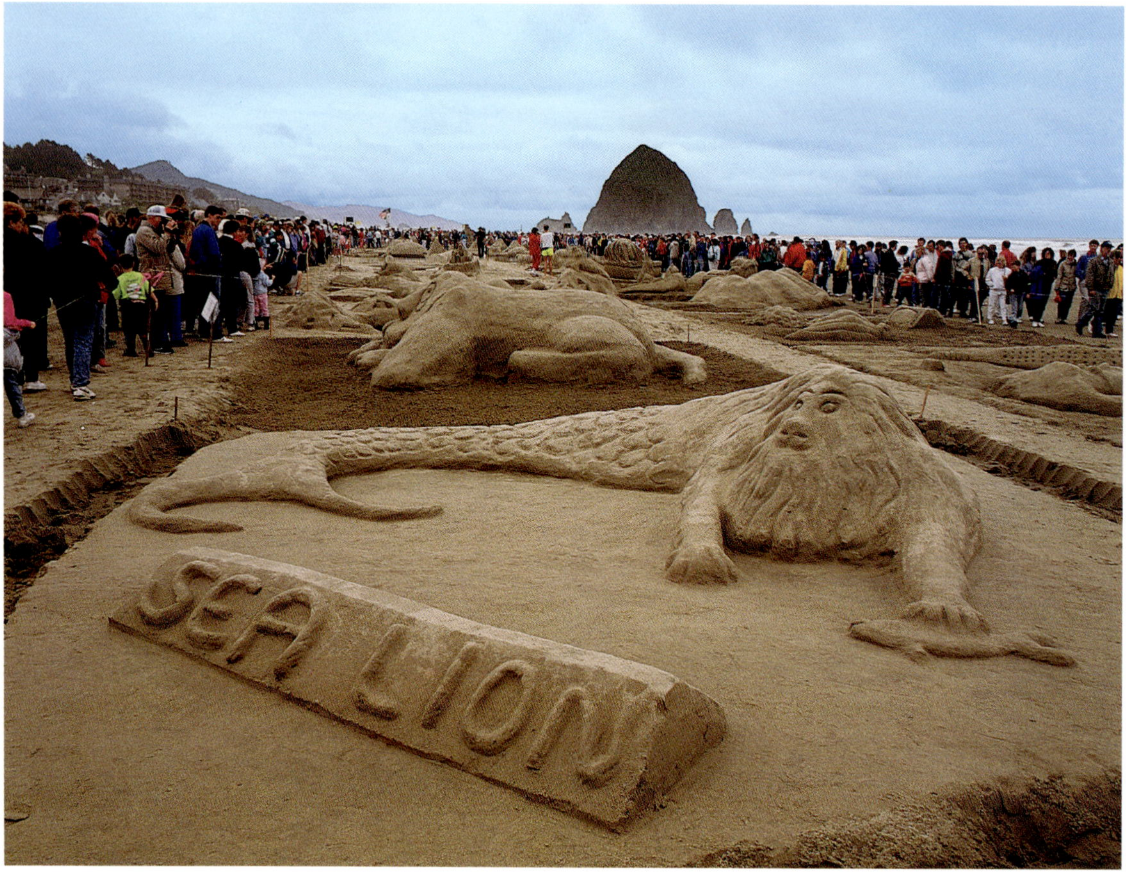

Sand Castle Day at Cannon Beach *(Northern Coast)* LARRY GEDDIS

Creativity reigns as hundreds of participants and thousands of spectators return each year for Sand Castle Day.

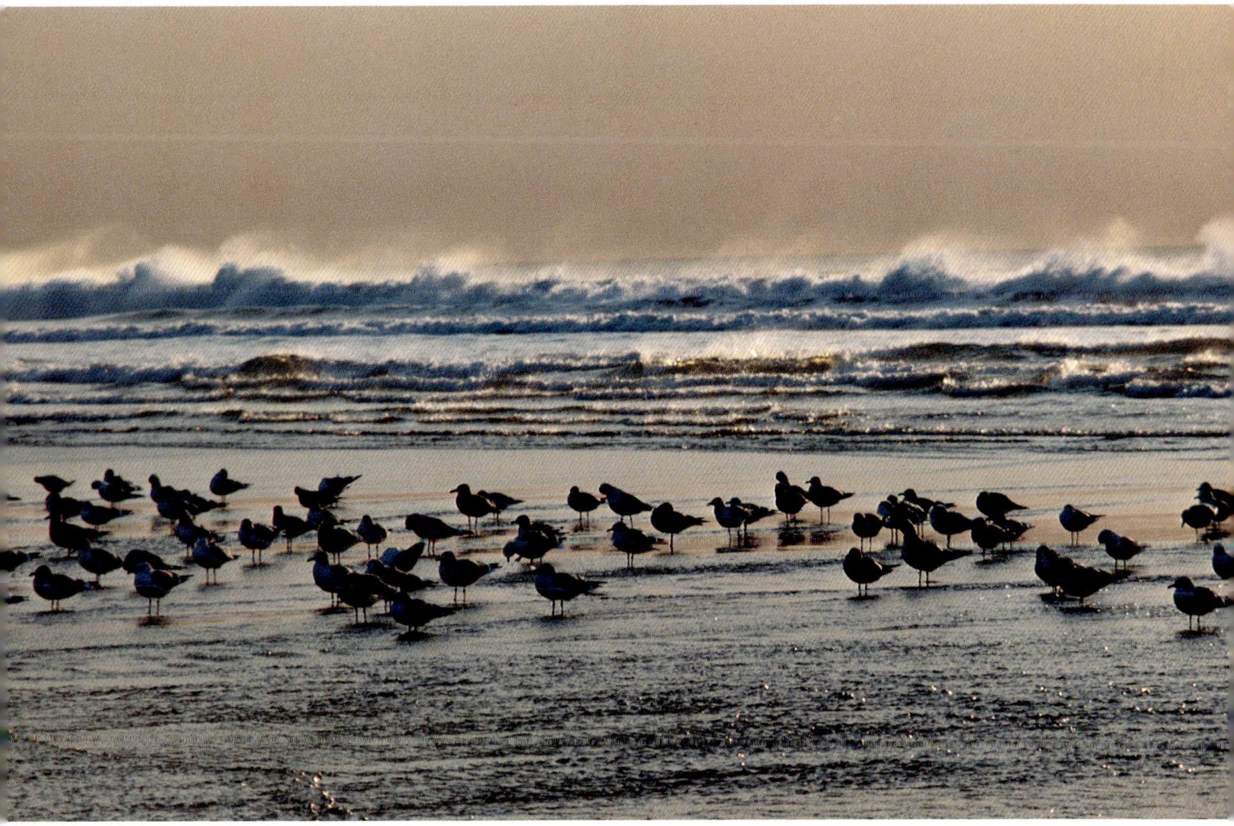

Seagulls gather near the crashing surf at Cannon Beach *(Northern Coast)* CHARLES JACOBS

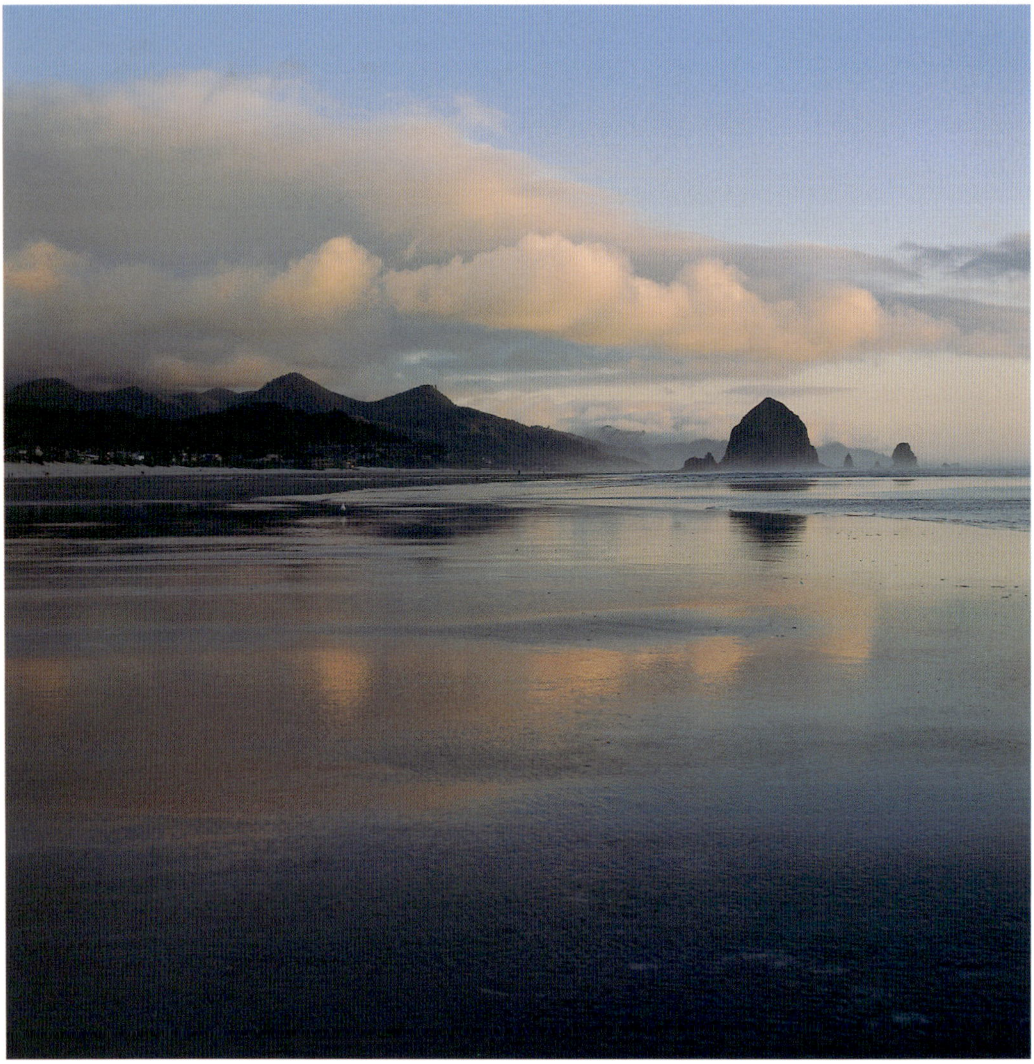

Haystack Rock and clouds are reflected at Cannon Beach
(Northern Coast) Charles Jacobs

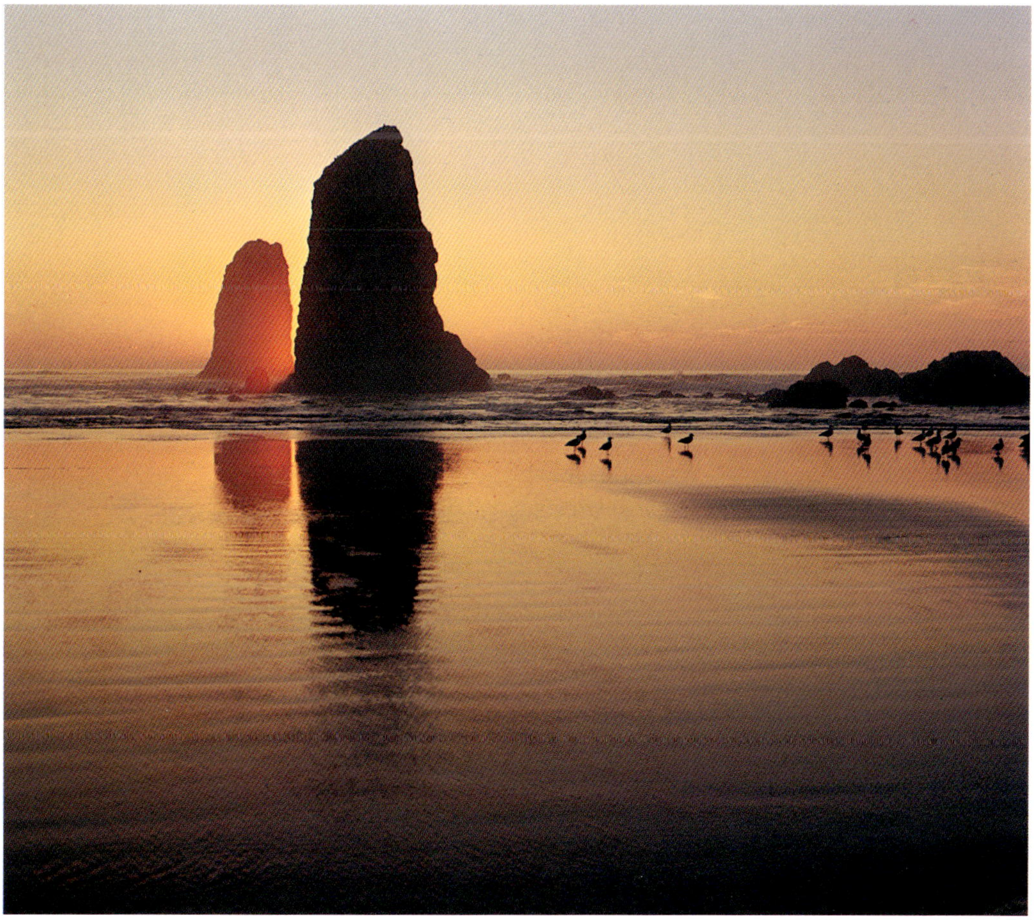

Sunset at Cannon Beach with the "Needles" *(Northern Coast)* Charles Jacobs

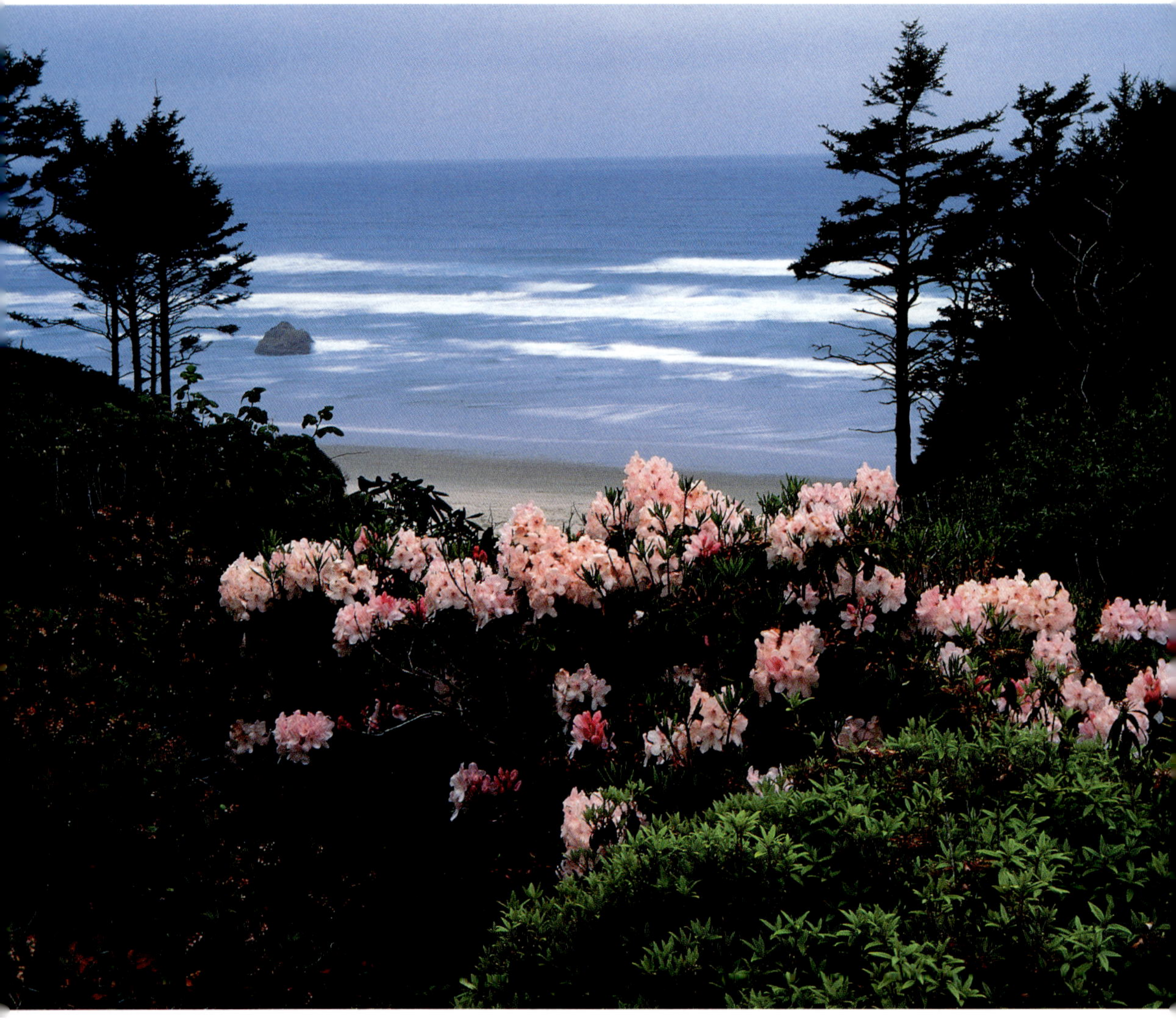

Wild rhododendrons bloom at Hug Point State Park *(Northern Coast)* STEVE TERRILL

Hug Point was so named because pioneer wagons had to dash between waves, hugging the point to get around on a narrow road blasted in the rock.

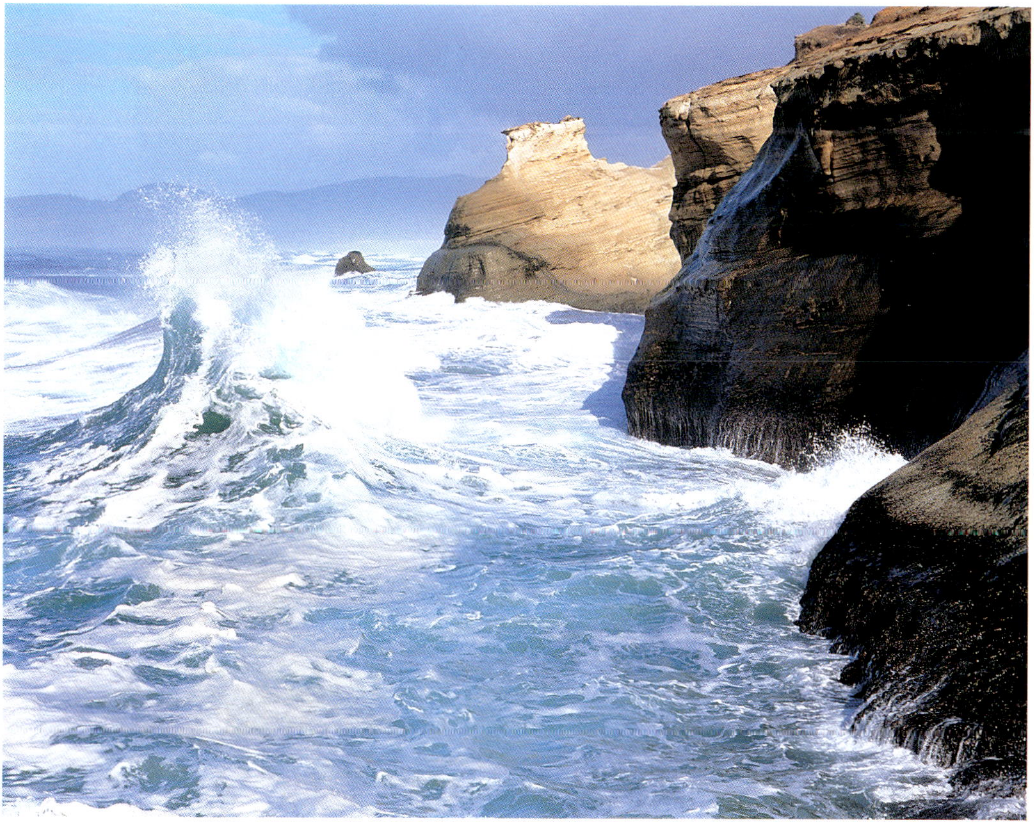

Stormy surf crashes against the sandstone cliffs of Cape Kiwanda, near Pacific City *(Northern Coast)* LARRY GEDDIS

Southernmost of the three headlands which make up the Three Capes Scenic Loop, Cape Kiwanda attracts hang gliders who often glide from the dunes just behind the cape.

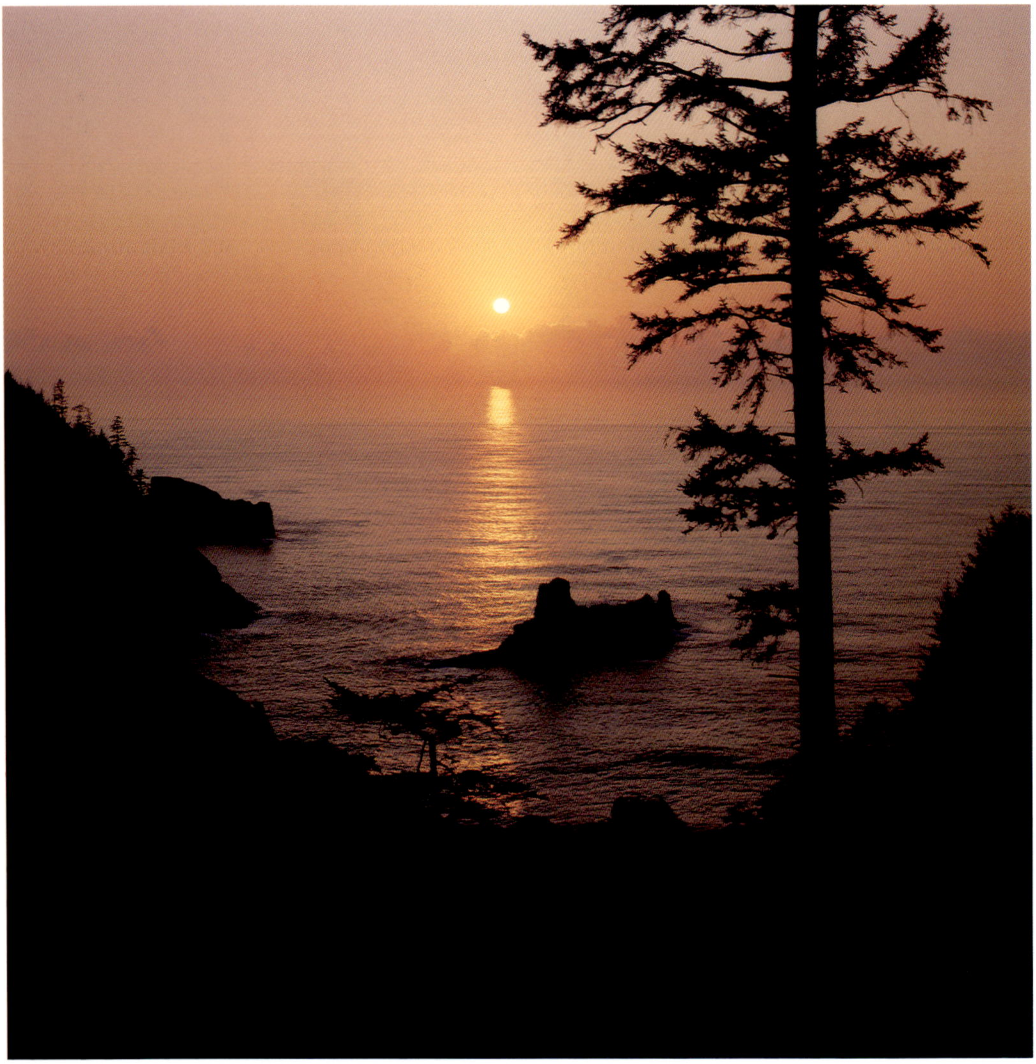

Sunset at Cape Lookout State Park *(Northern Coast)* Charles Jacobs

One of the most prominent headlands on the coast, it juts almost two miles into the sea and is a popular year-round state campground.

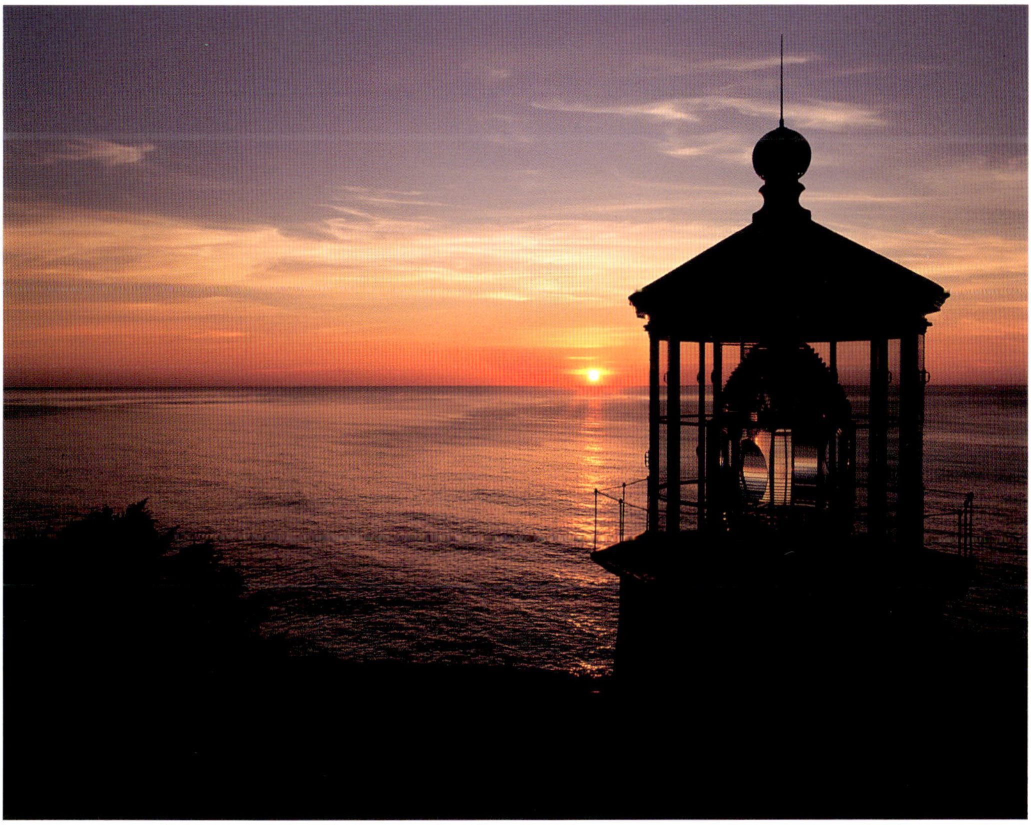

Winter sunset silhouettes the century-old Cape Meares Lighthouse
(Northern Coast) LARRY GEDDIS

In Cape Meares State Park, trails lead through the rain forest to the Octopus Tree and to the historic 1890 lighthouse at the tip of the headland.

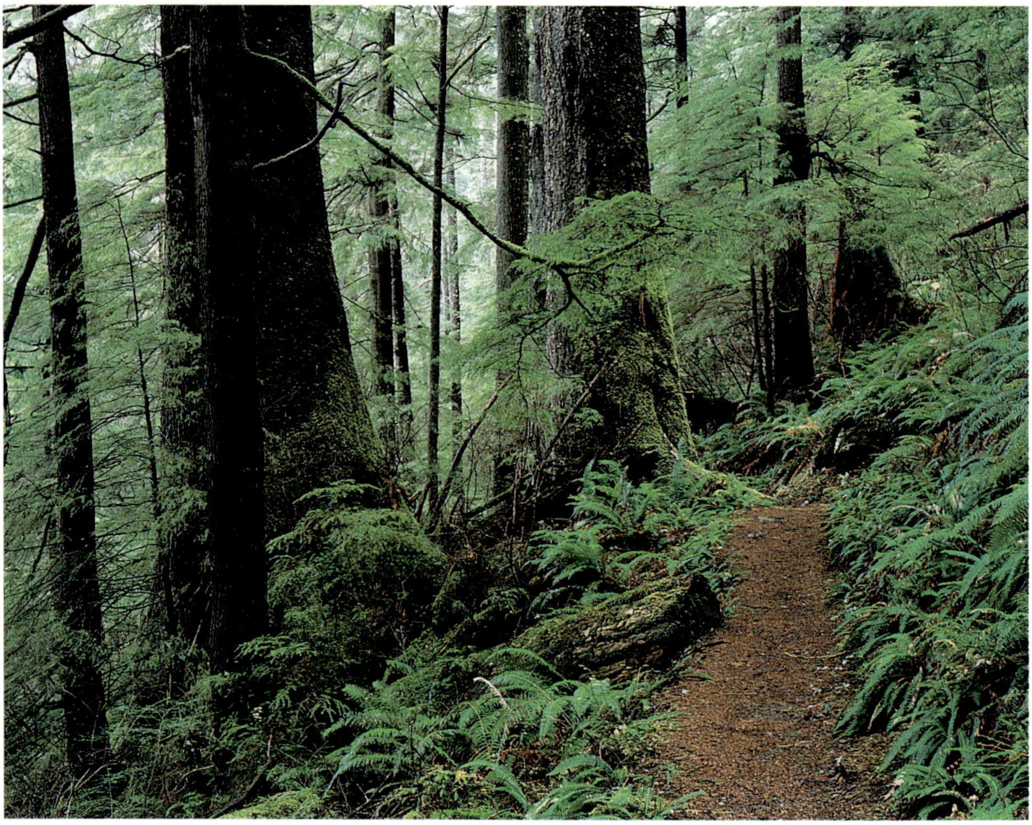

Trail to Cascade Head *(Central Coast)* LARRY GEDDIS

Though much of Cascade Head is protected as a scenic research center by The Nature Conservancy, hikers can sample it on several trails which pass through an old growth forest of Sitka spruce and western hemlock.

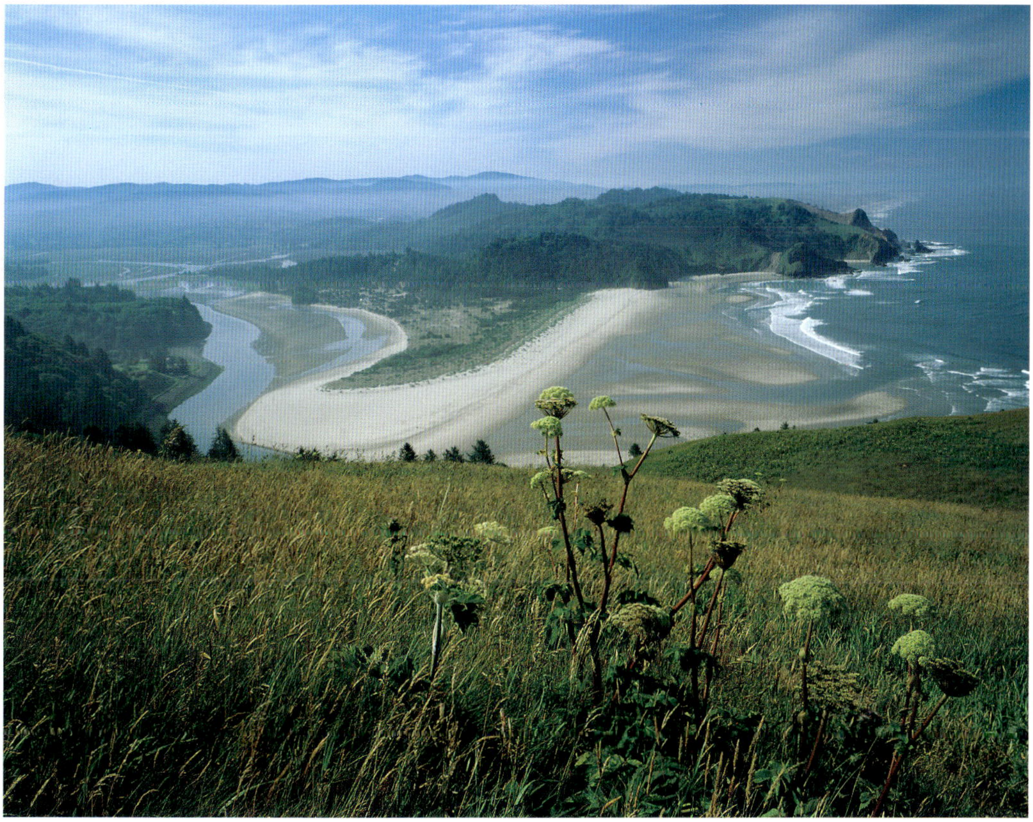

Cascade Head, looking south, where the Salmon River winds its way to the sea
(Central Coast) Steve Terrill

Wildflower meadows, gentle dunes, and coastal forests merge in this dramatic landscape.

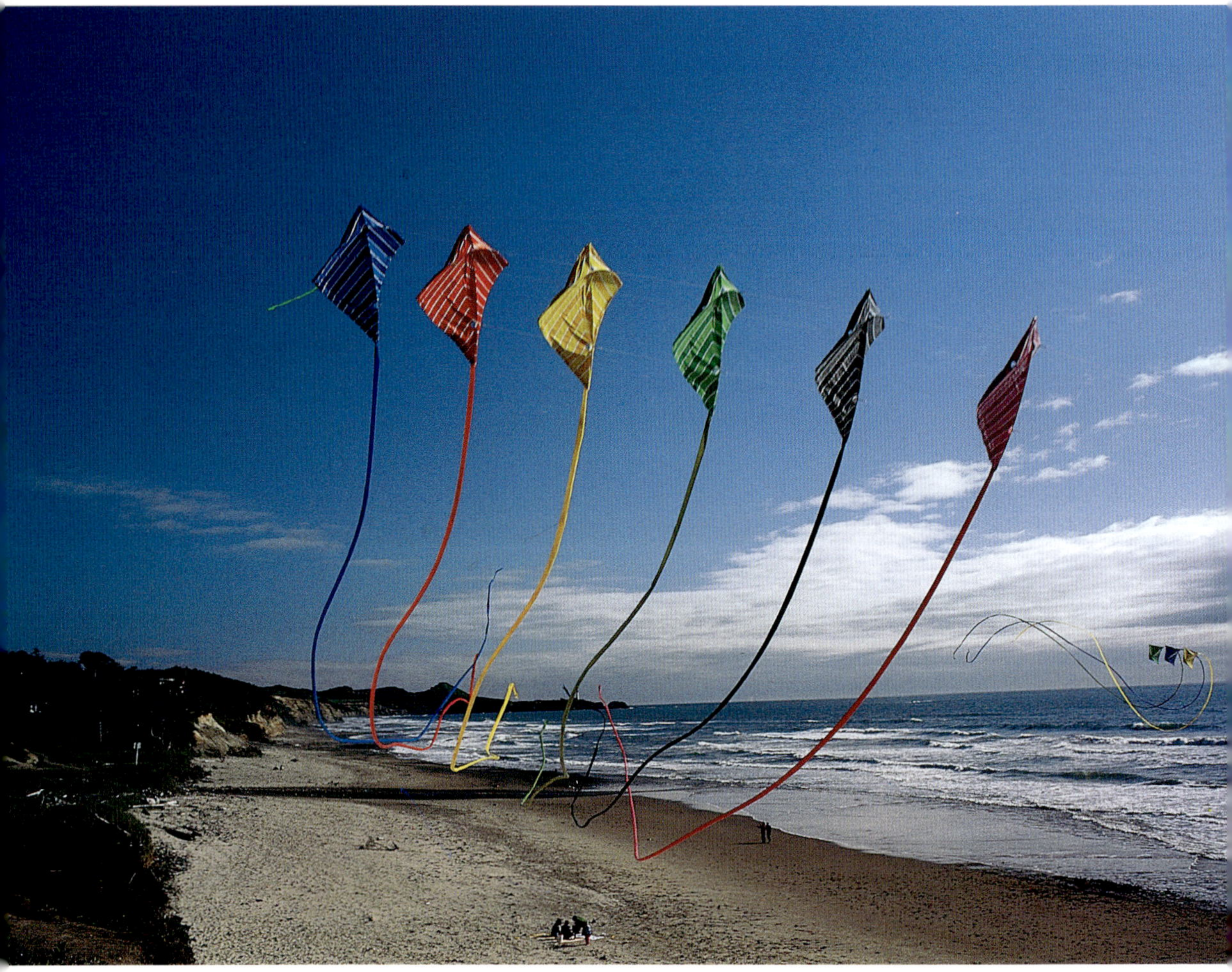

Kites take flight over Beverly Beach State Park *(Central Coast)* STEVE TERRILL

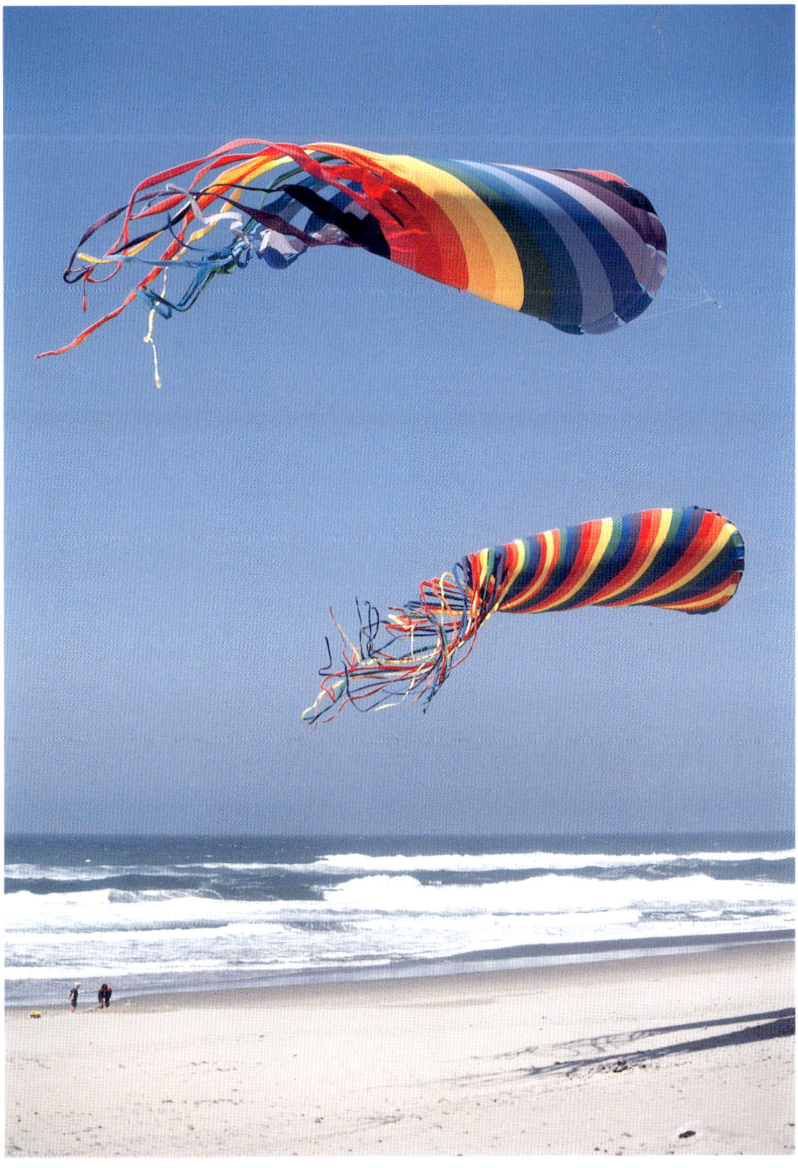

Ocean breezes fill colorful kites at Oregon's Kite Capital, Lincoln City *(Central Coast)* CHARLES JACOBS

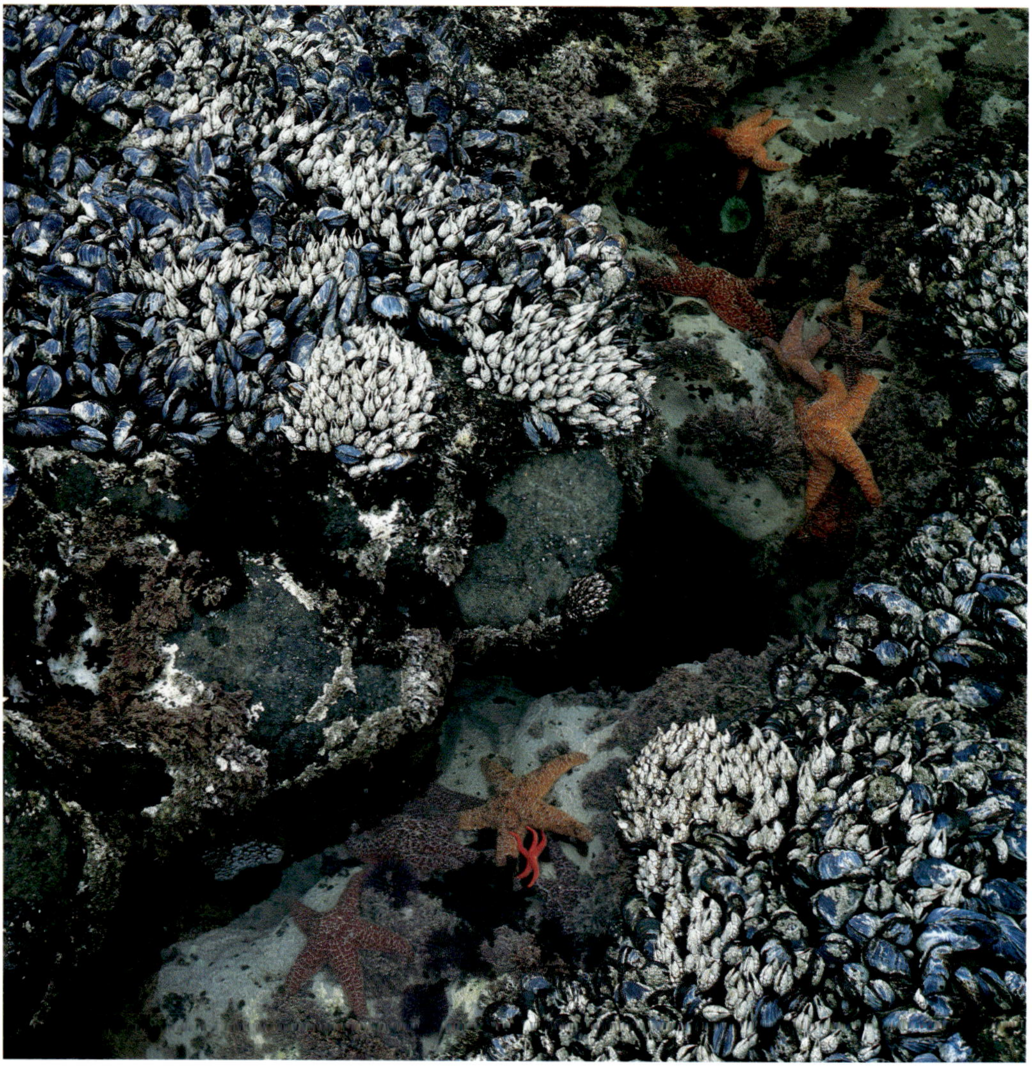

Tidepool community at Yaquina Head *(Central Coast)* STEVE TERRILL

Abundant starfish, sea anemone, and mussels can be seen here.

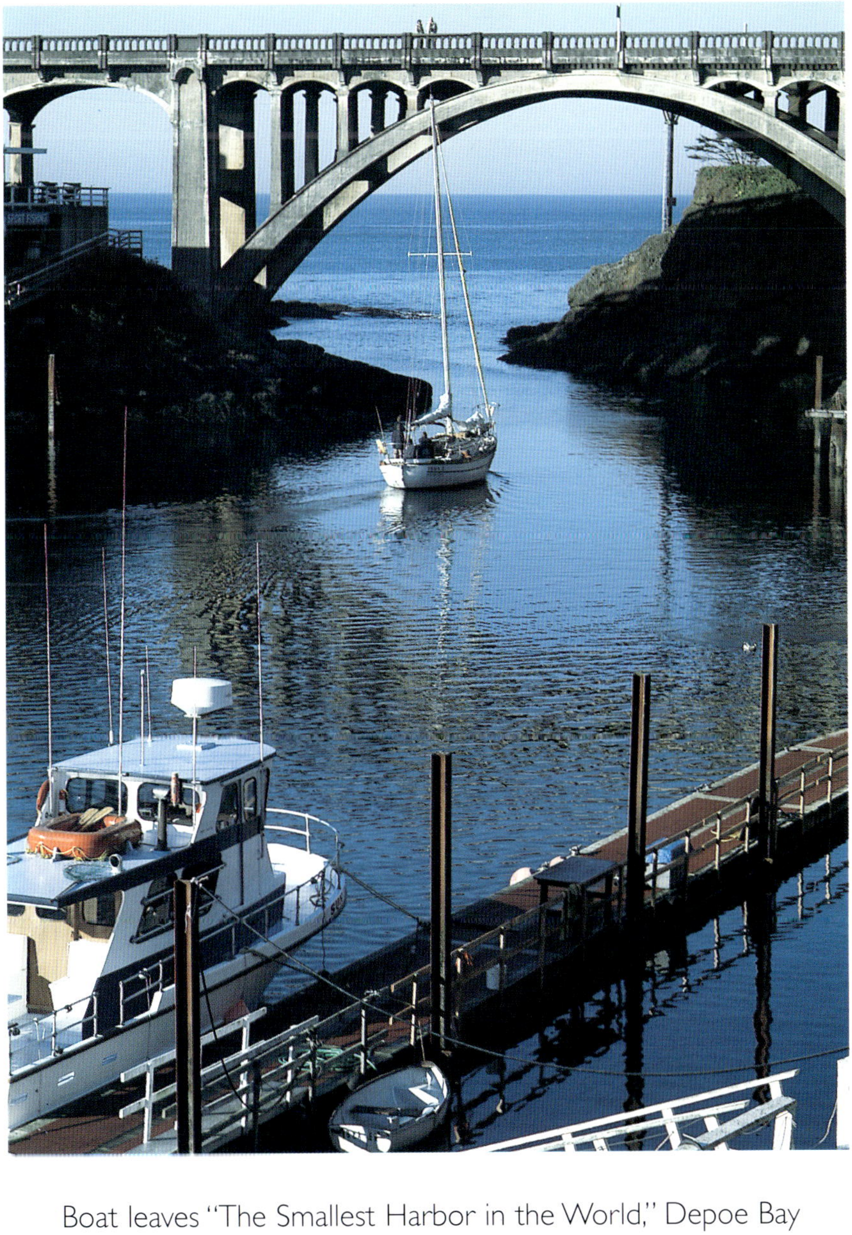

Boat leaves "The Smallest Harbor in the World," Depoe Bay
(Central Coast) ANNE JACOBS

Sightseeing, charter fishing, and whale watching excursions depart from this harbor each day.

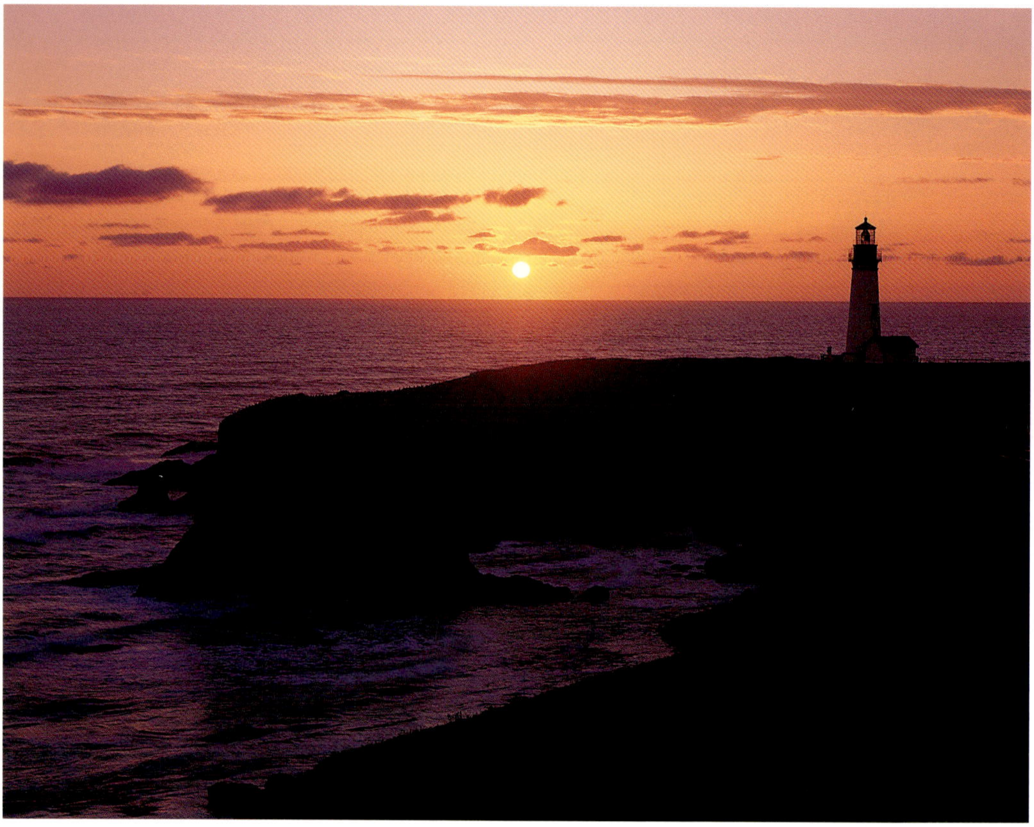

Built in 1873, the Yaquina Head Lighthouse with a beautiful winter sunset
(Central Coast) STEVE TERRILL

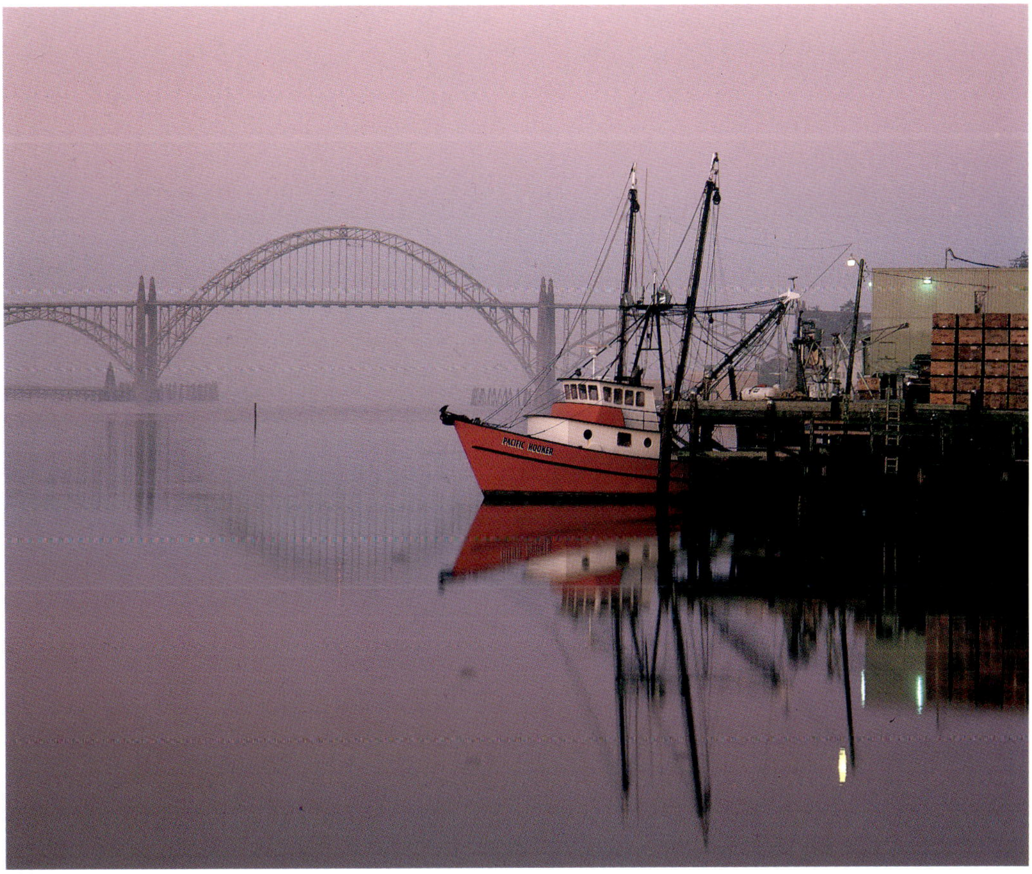

A foggy morning reflection of Yaquina Bay Bridge and a fishing trawler at Newport *(Central Coast)* STEVE TERRILL

The picturesque bay front includes charter fishing boats, canneries, numerous shops, the Hatfield Marine Science Center and the Oregon Coast Aquarium.

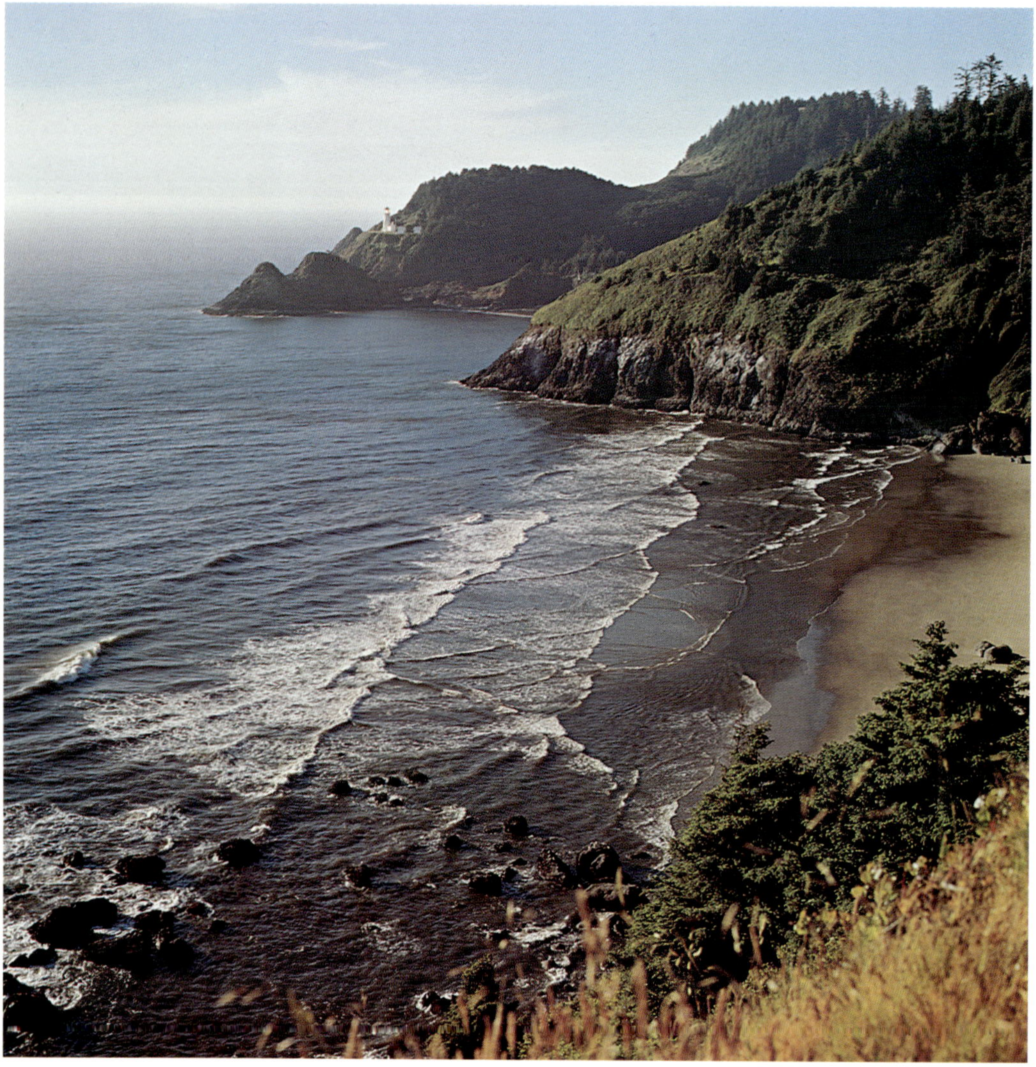

Surf rolls in with Heceta Head Lighthouse in the distance
(Central Coast) CHARLES JACOBS

Heceta Head was named for the Spanish sea captain Bruno Heceta, who sailed along the Oregon coast in 1775.

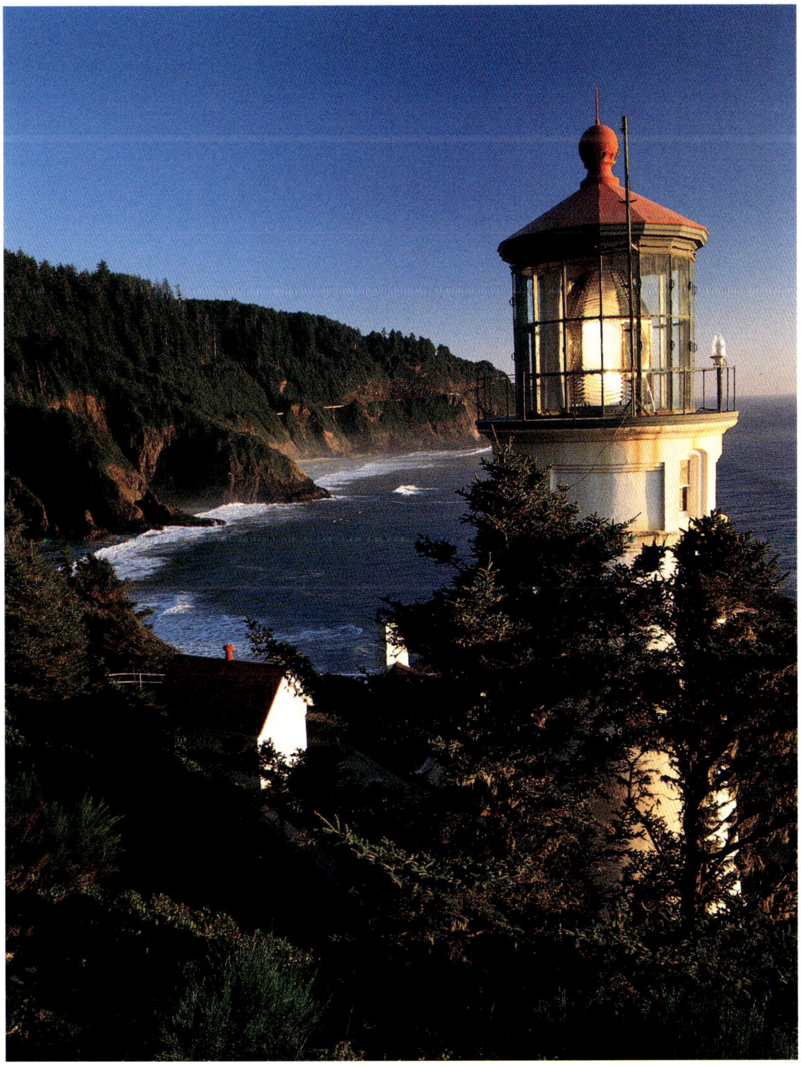

Heceta Head Lighthouse, built in 1893, is part of Devil's Elbow State Park *(Central Coast)* LARRY GEDDIS

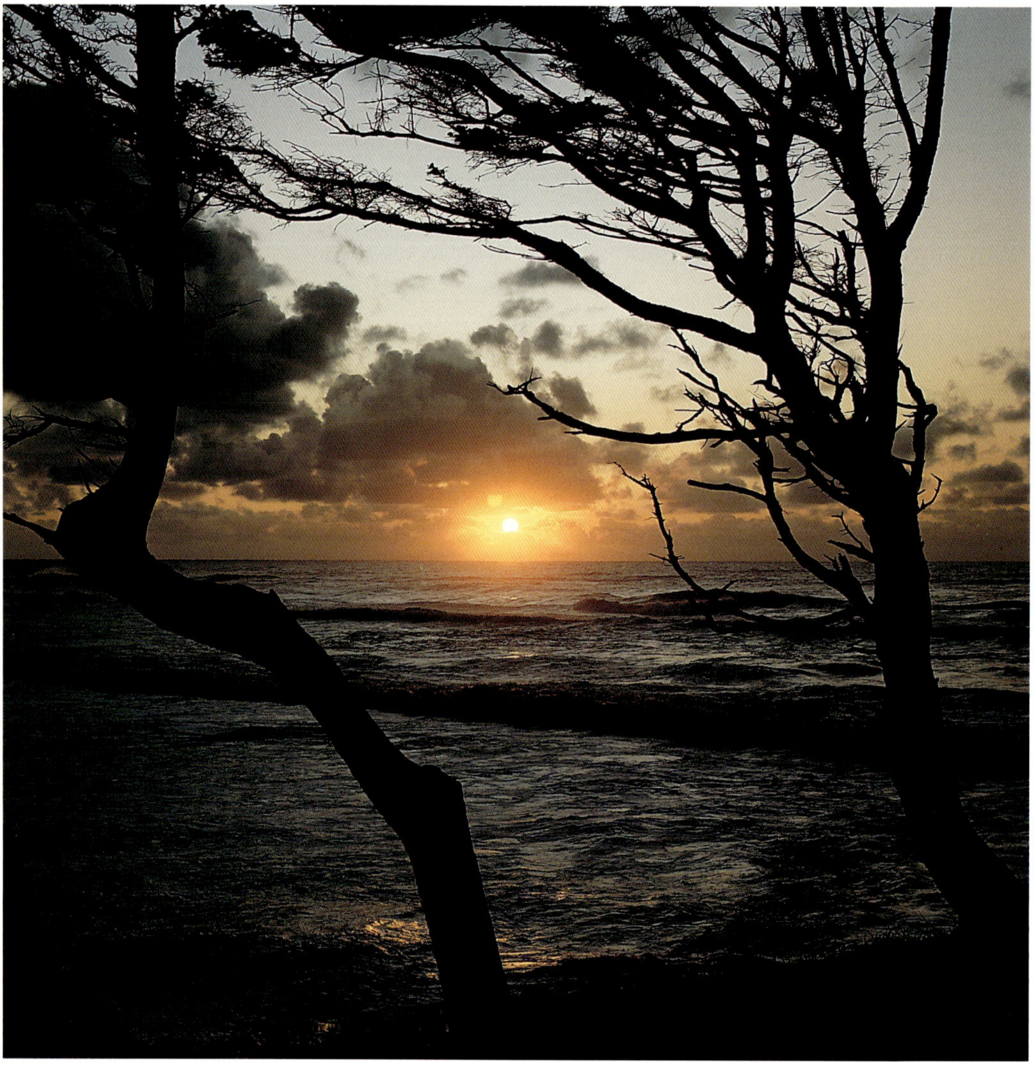

Pacific sunset silhouettes the Siuslaw National Forest at Cape Perpetua
(Central Coast) CHARLES JACOBS

British navigator, James Cook, discovered the cape in 1778 and named it for the martyred St. Perpetua. Today, ten miles of trails offer access for exploring the unique ecosystem of this area.

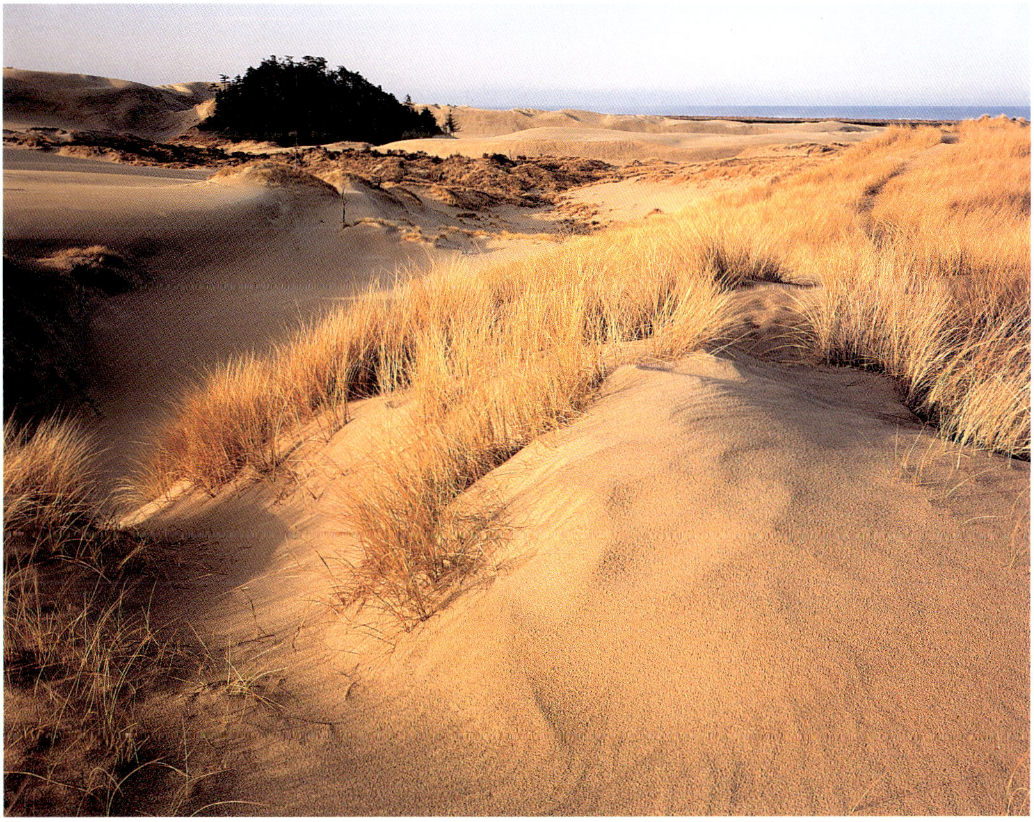

Morning light on sand dunes at Oregon Dunes National Recreation Area
(Central Coast) Steve Terrill

Protected by Congressional action in 1972, the Oregon Dunes National Recreation Area includes more than 32,000 acres of coastal dunes.

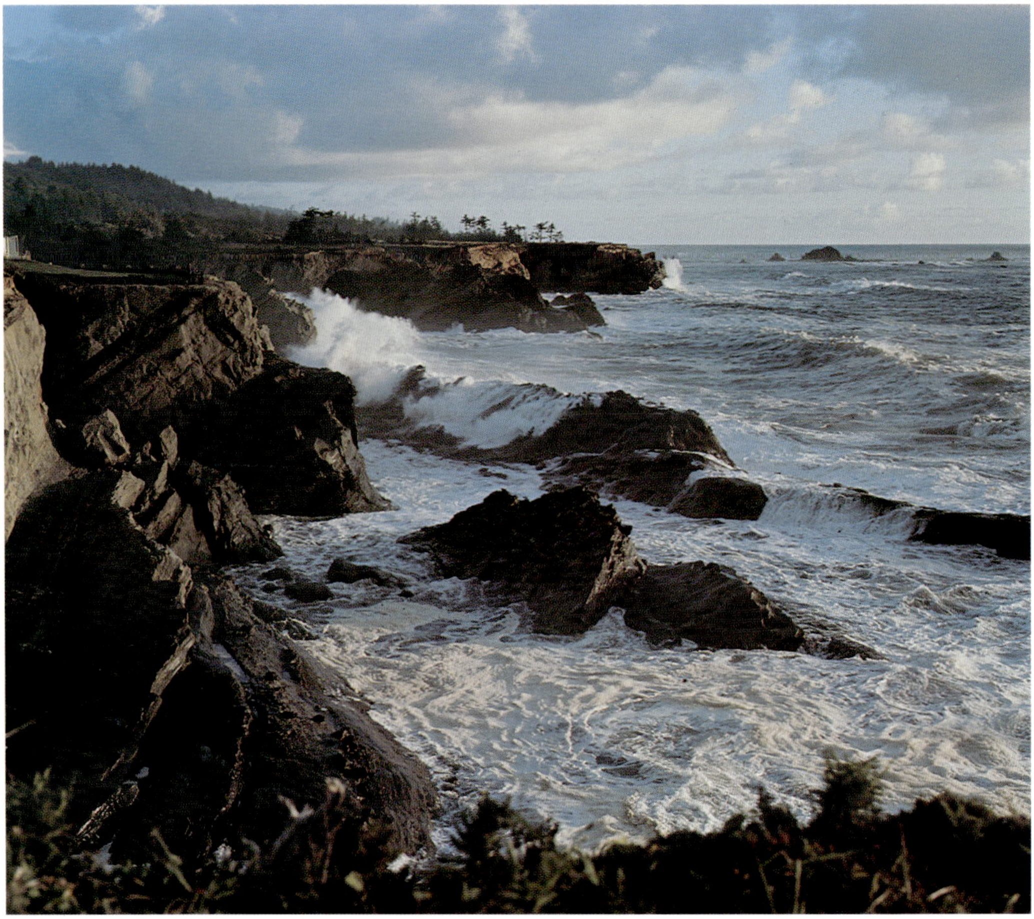

Evening light on the pounding surf at Shore Acres State Park
(Southern Coast) Charles Jacobs

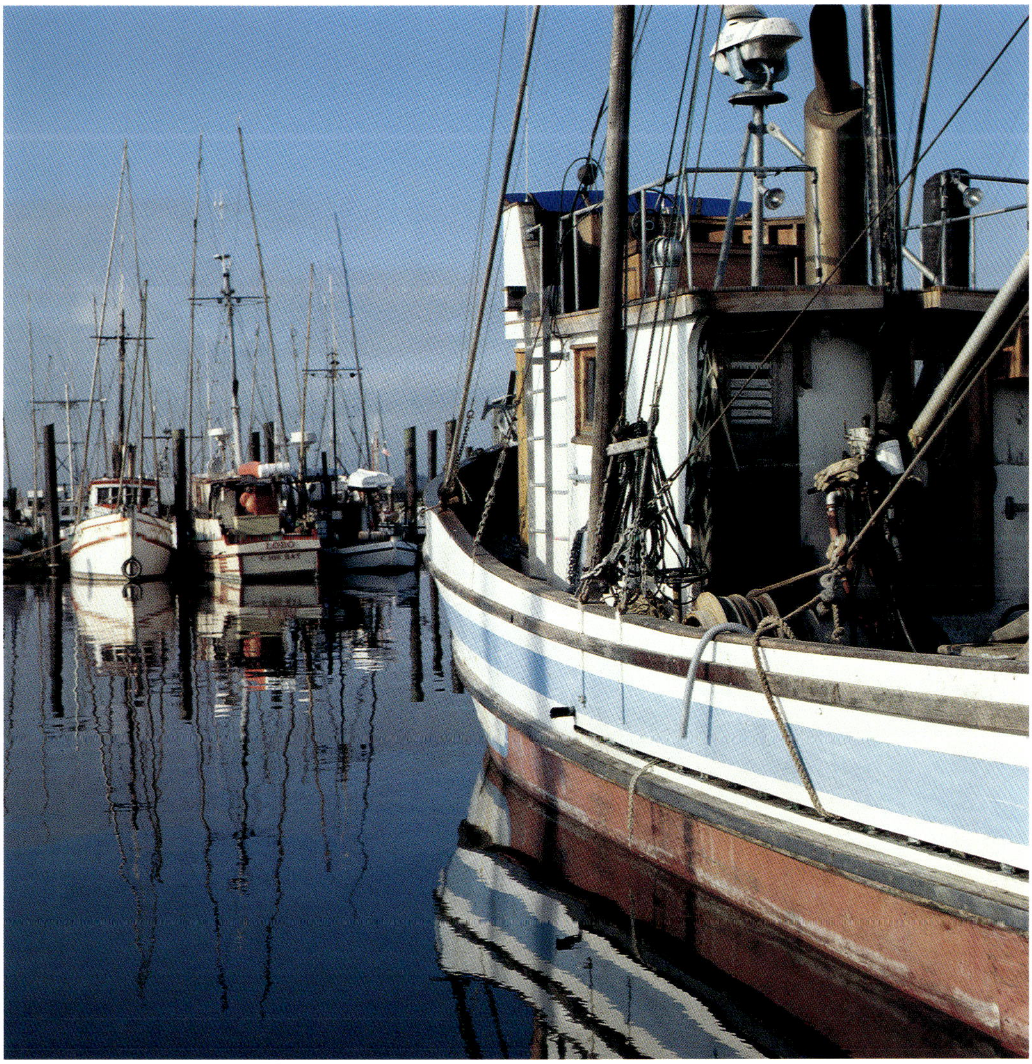

Fishing boats cast a warm reflection on Charleston Harbor
(Southern Coast) CHARLES JACOBS

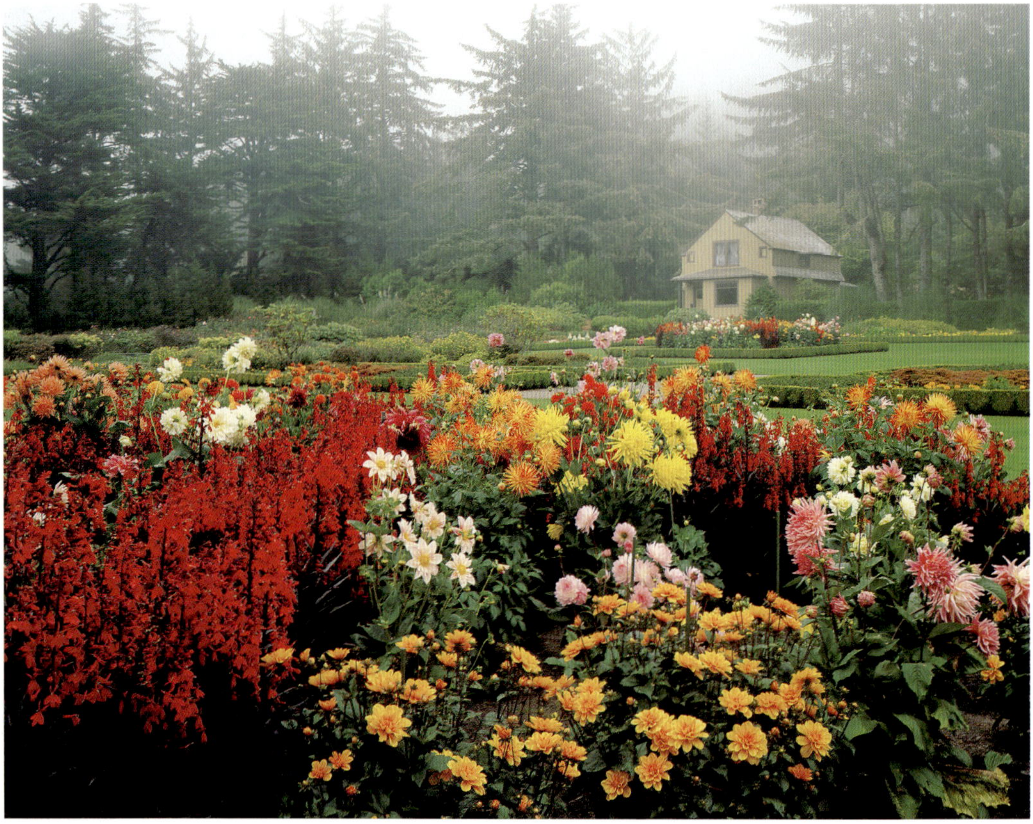

Formal Garden, Shore Acres State Park *(Southern Coast)* STEVE TERRILL

Once the estate of lumber and shipping magnate, Louis Simpson, the park combines spectacular oceanfront scenery with formal gardens. Many of the original plants were imported from around the world on lumber schooners built at his North Bend shipyards.

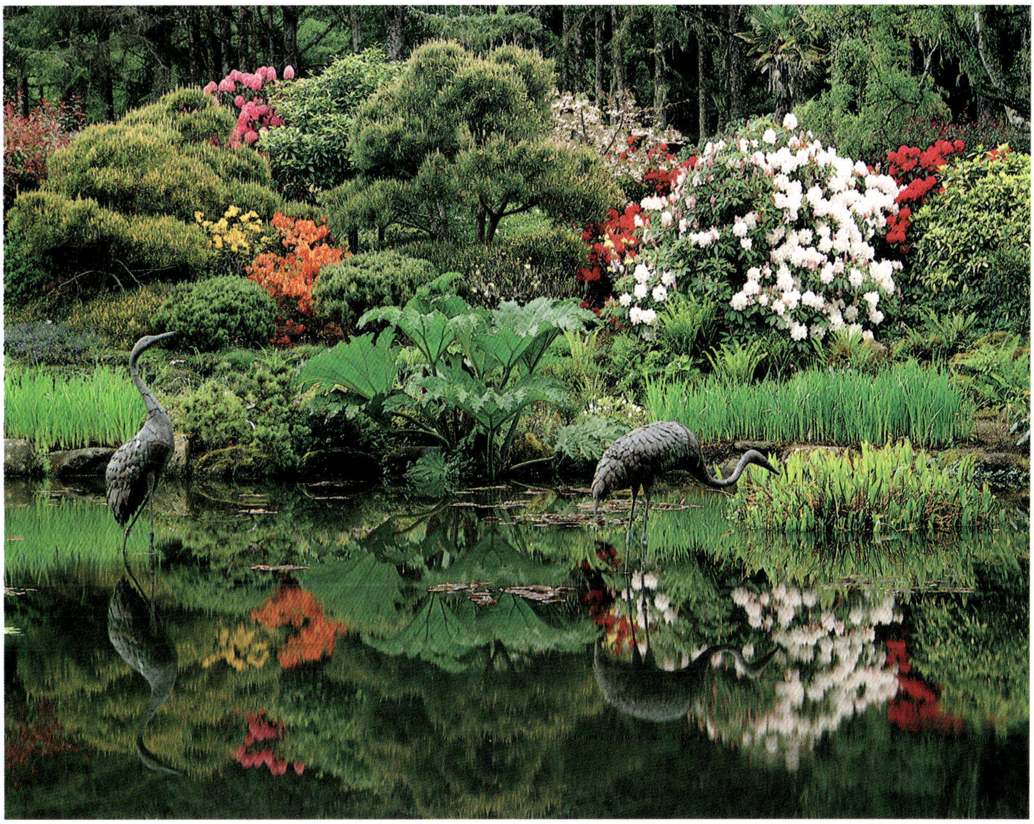

Spring bloom at the botanical garden of Shore Acres State Park
(Southern Coast) STEVE TERRILL

Following Pages:
A Pacific breaker explodes against the sandstone cliffs at Shore Acres State Park
(Southern Coast) LARRY GEDDIS

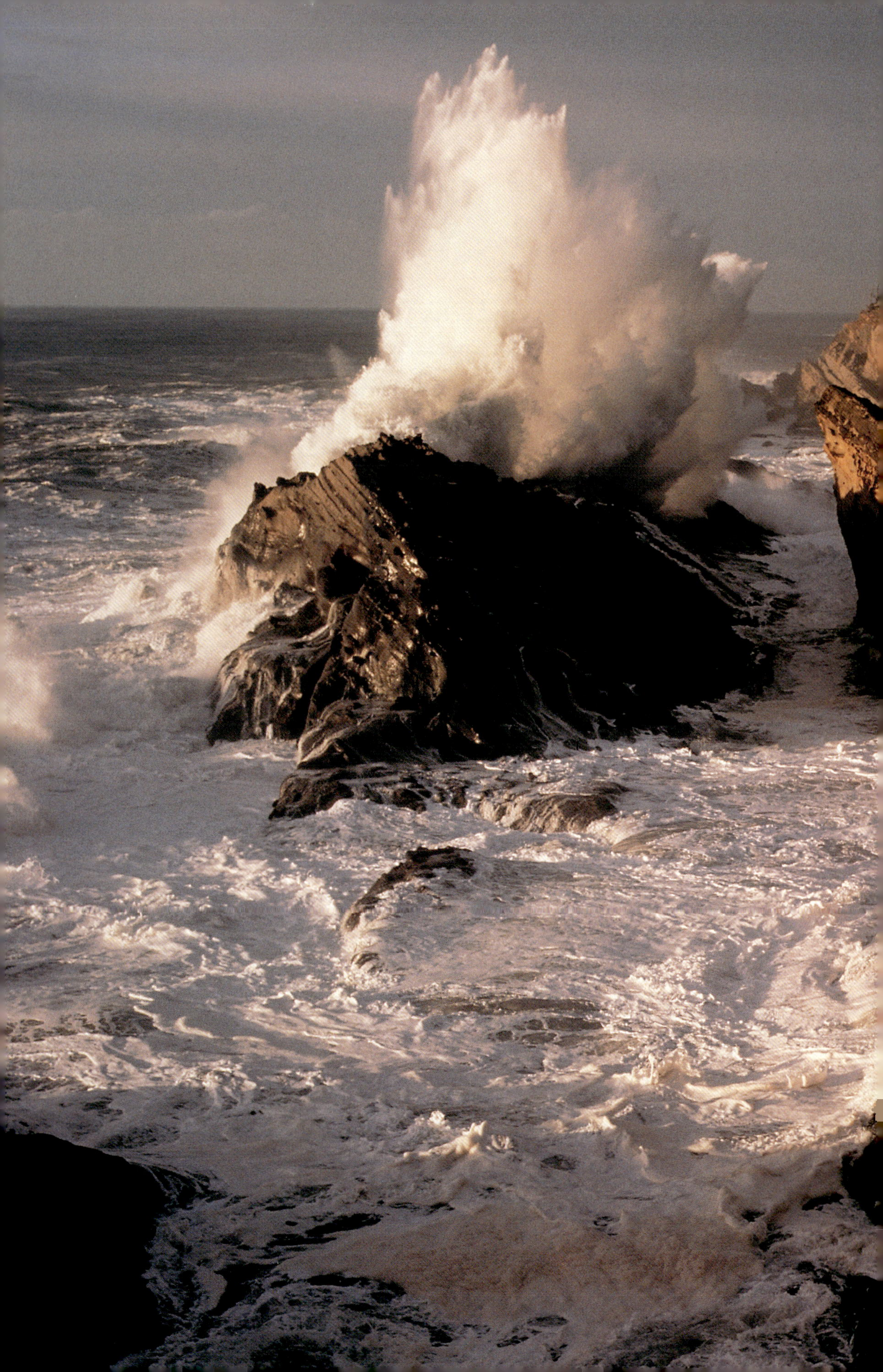

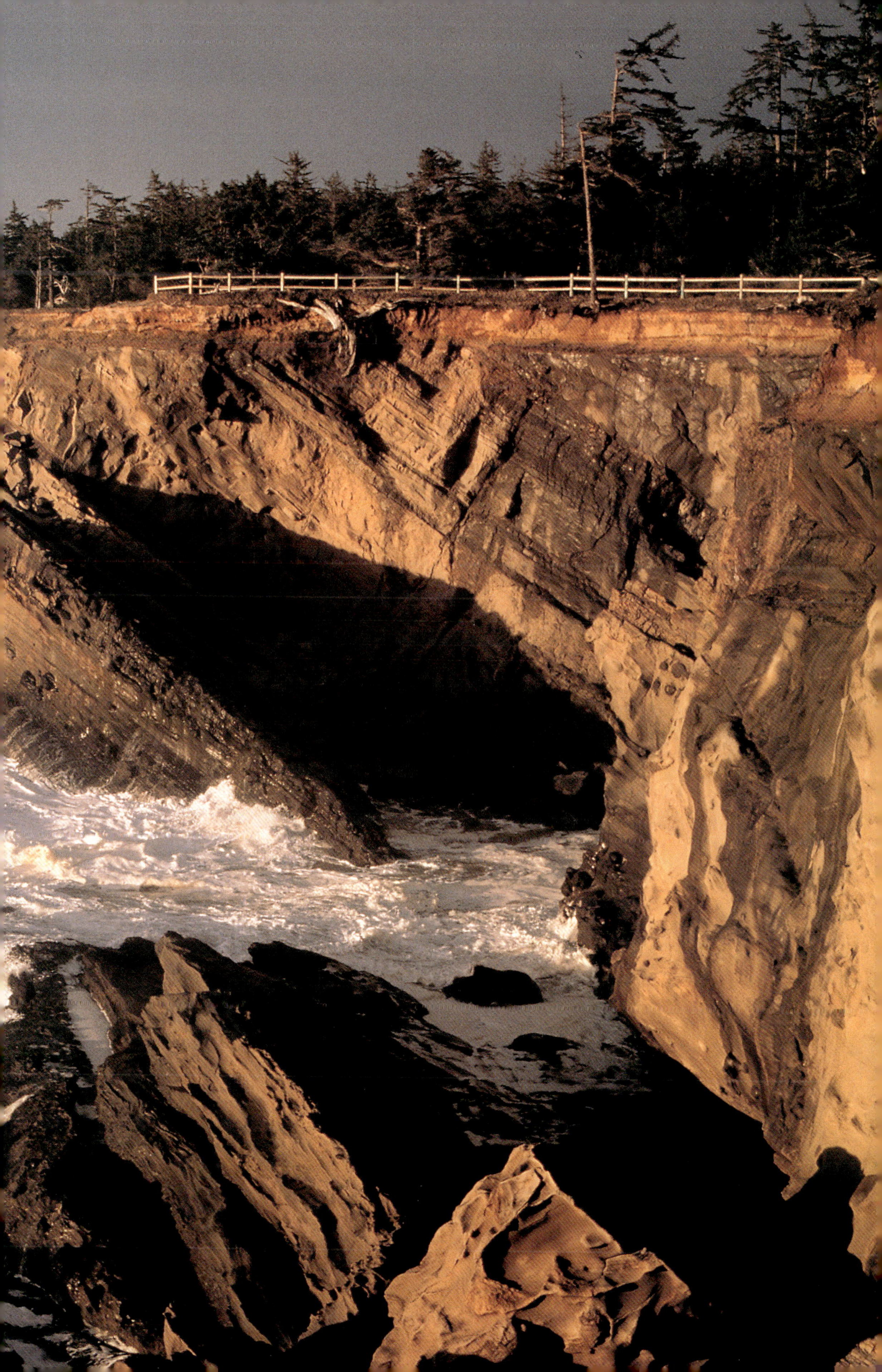

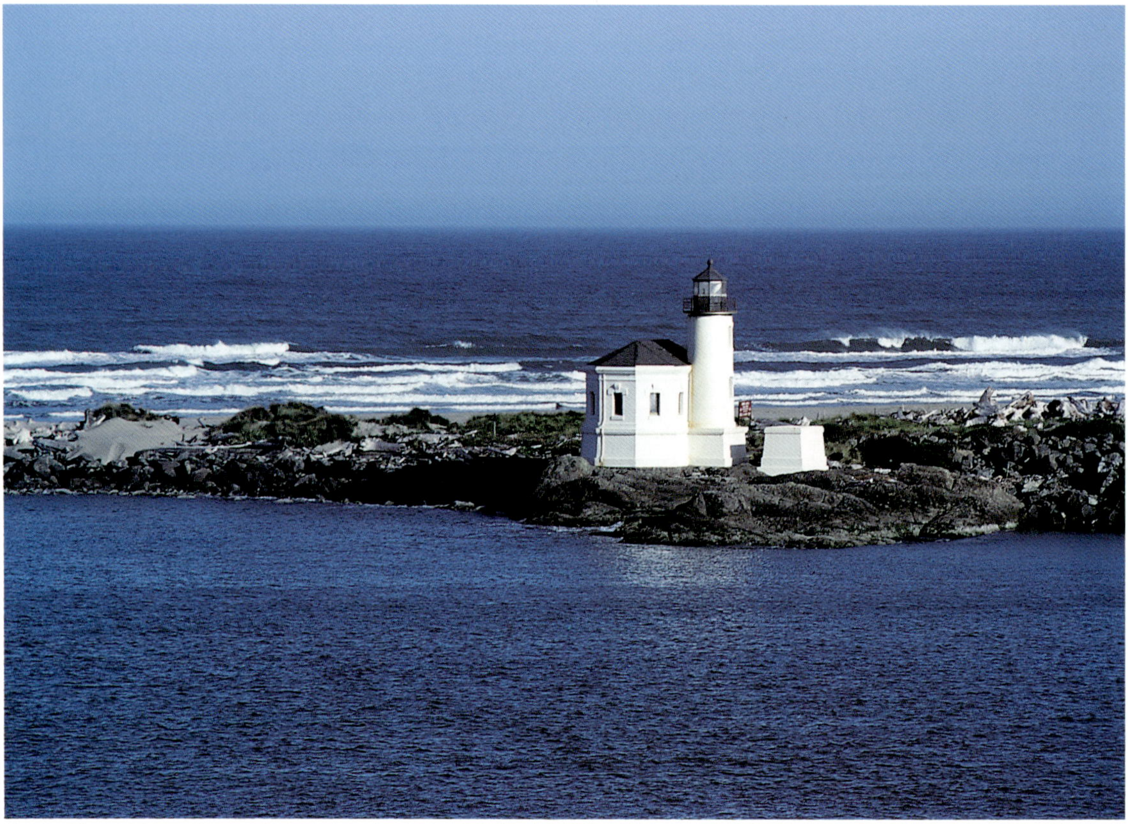

Coquille River Lighthouse at Bandon *(Southern Coast)* Charles Jacobs

Built in 1896, the lighthouse was one of the few structures left standing after Bandon's disastrous 1936 fire.

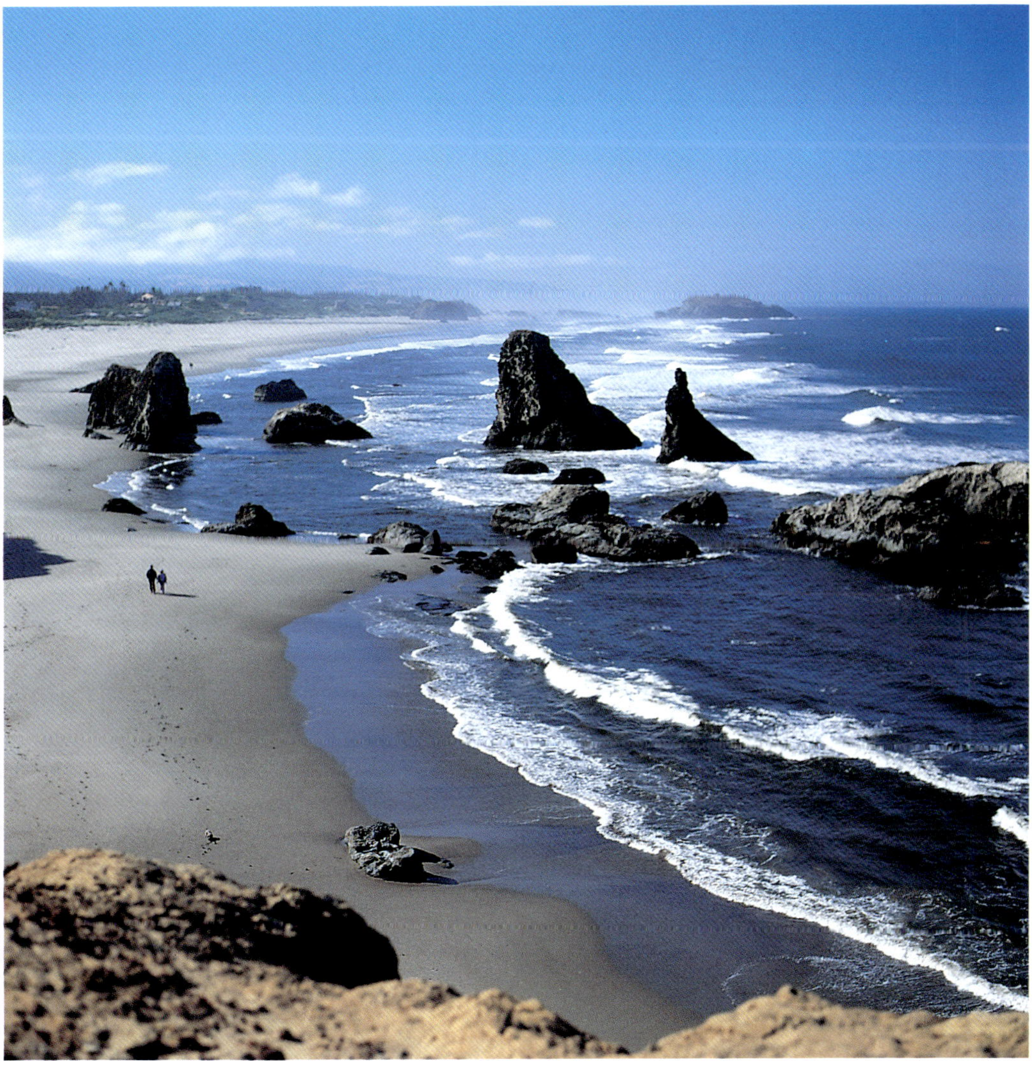

From Bandon Wayside State Park, a grand view of the many offshore sea stacks along Bandon Beach *(Southern Coast)* CHARLES JACOBS

Along with the magnificent rock formations, Bandon is famous for being "Oregon's Cranberry Capital" and the "Storm-watching Capital of the World."

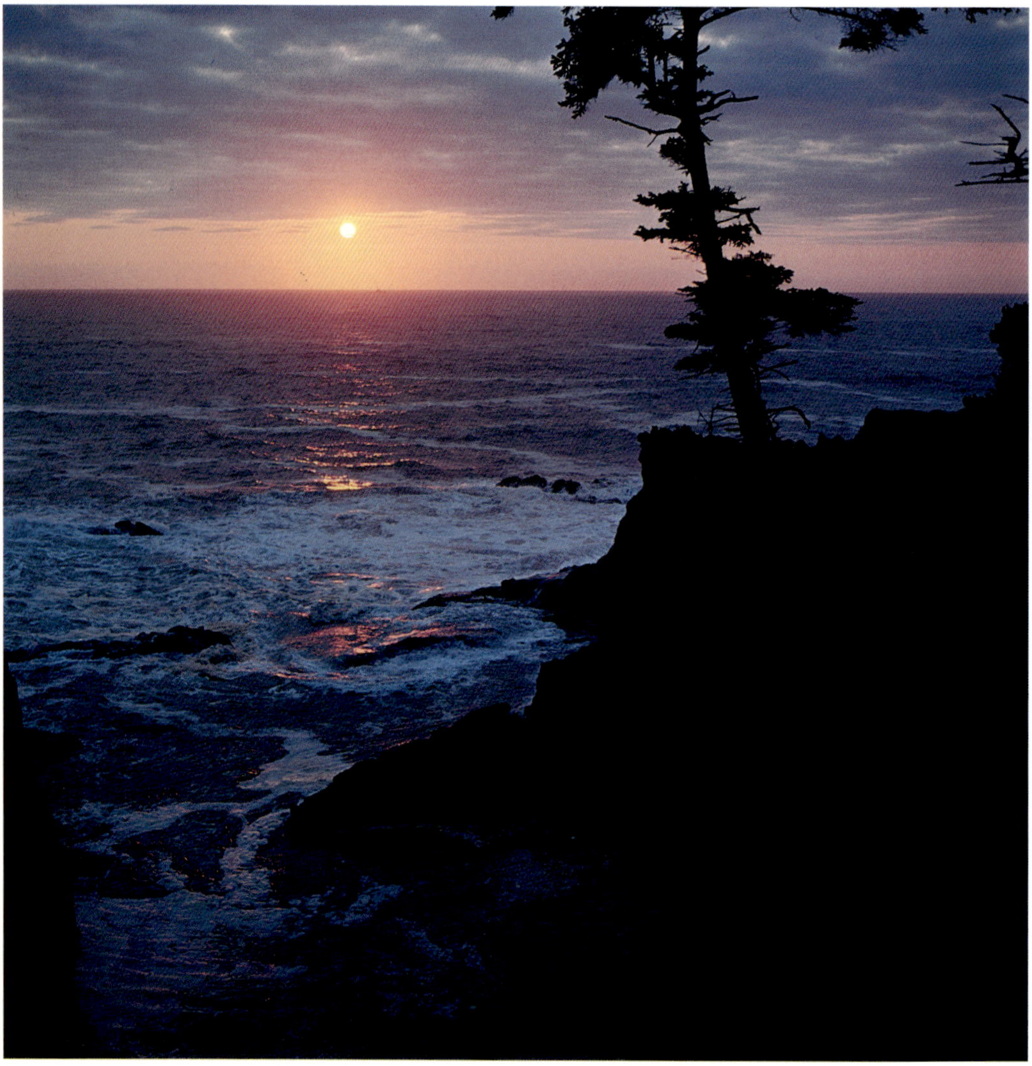

Autumn sunset at Shore Acres State Park *(Southern Coast)* CHARLES JACOBS

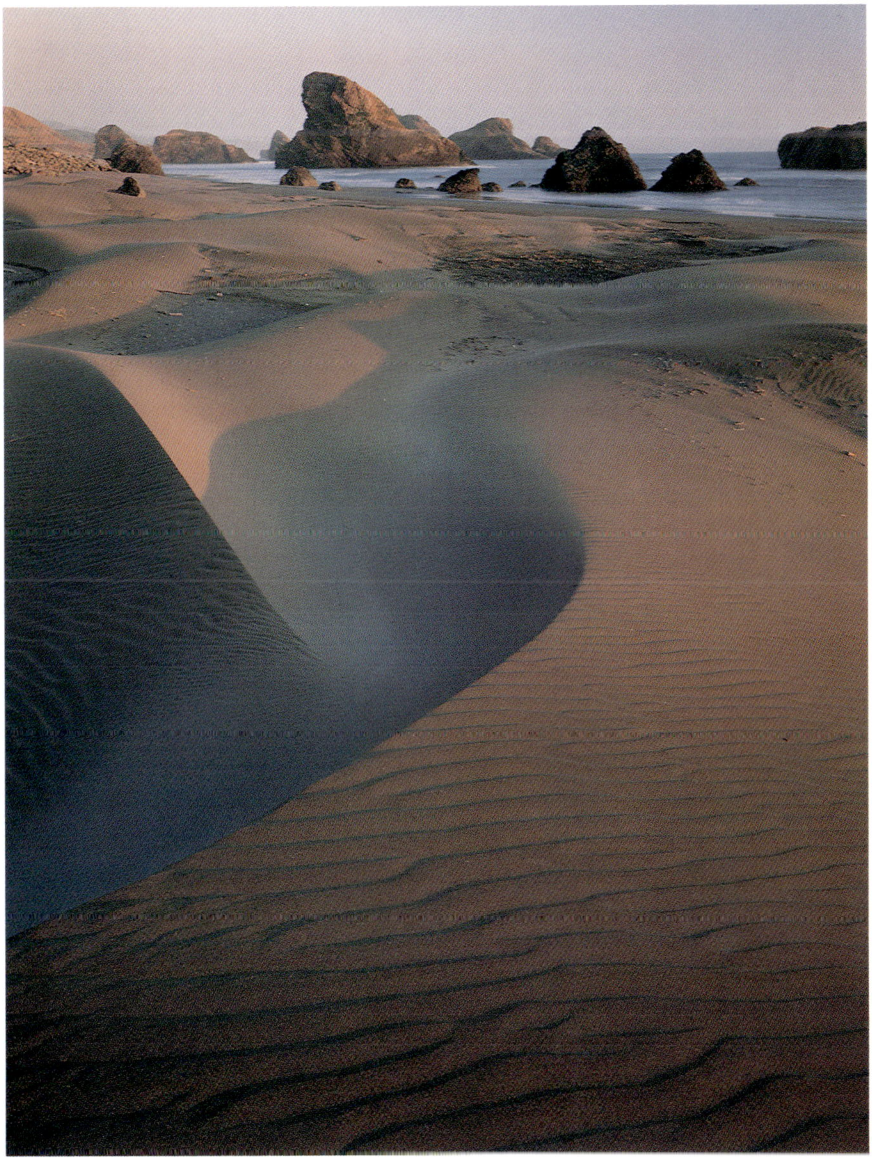

Early morning light on the sand dunes at Cape Sebastian
(Southern Coast) STEVE TERRILL

U.S. Highway 101 hugs the coast along this rugged and wild section, providing outstanding views.

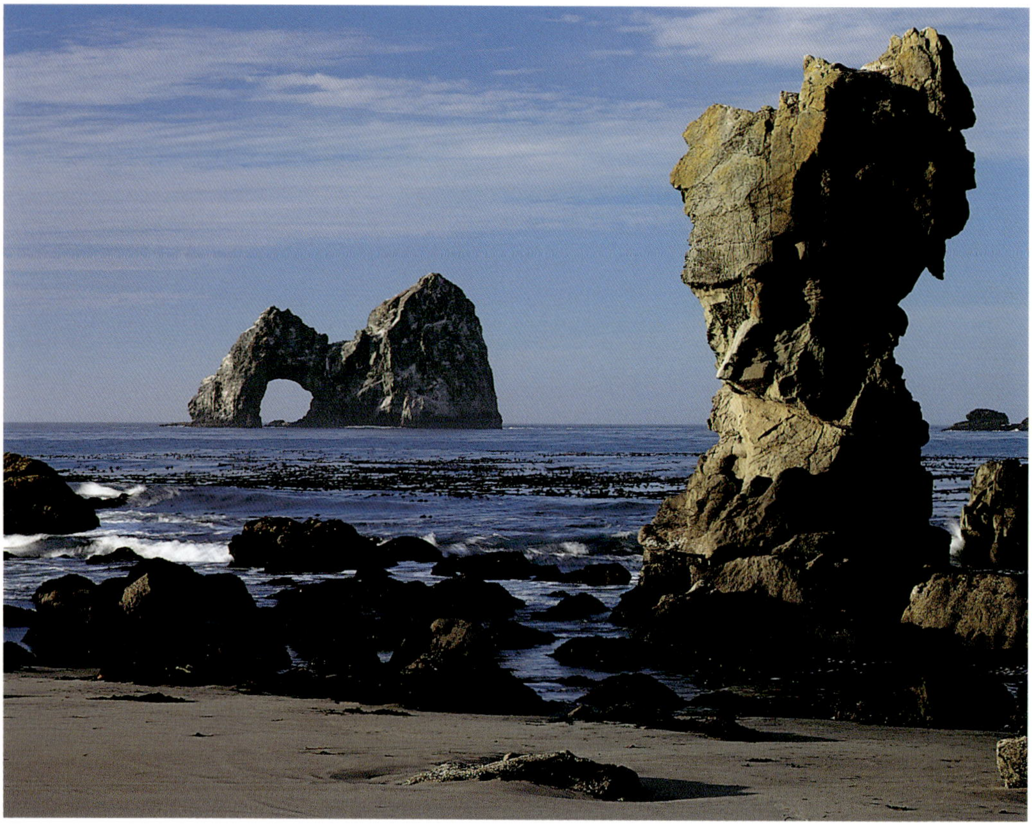

(Southern Coast) Larry Geddis

There are many unique rock formations on Oregon's southern coastline, including the 325-foot-high Mack Arch and Crook Rock.

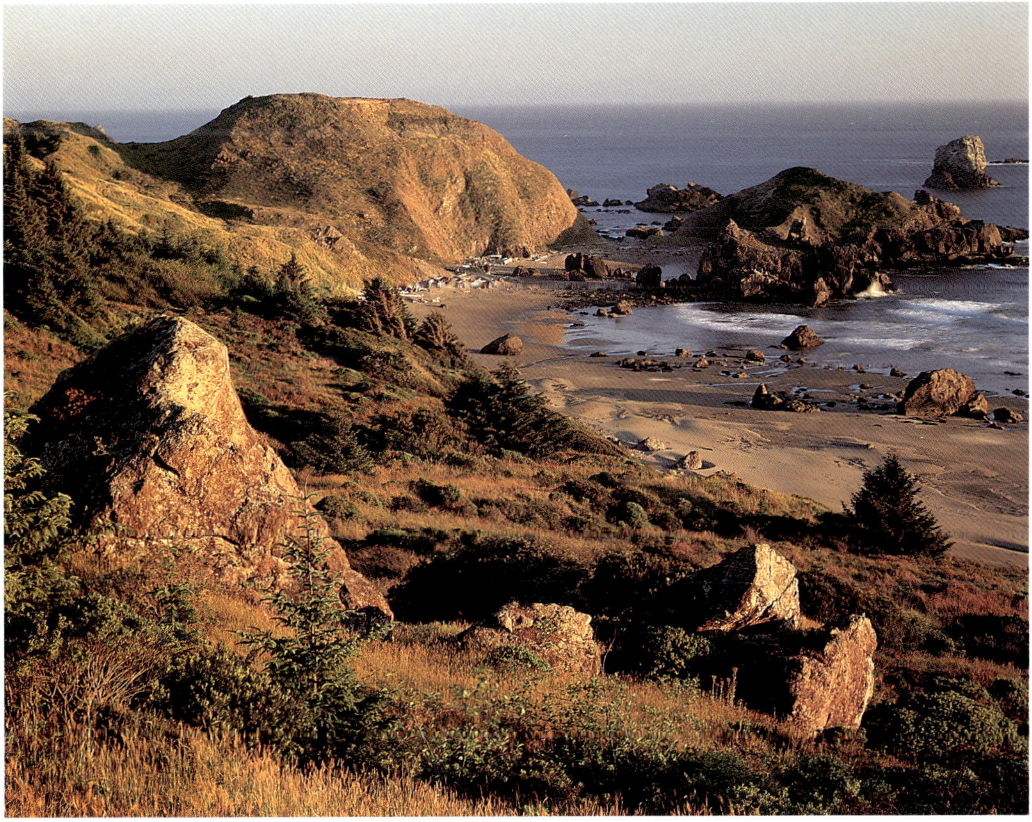

Late evening light at Lone Ranch Beach in Boardman State Park
(Southern Coast) STEVE TERRILL

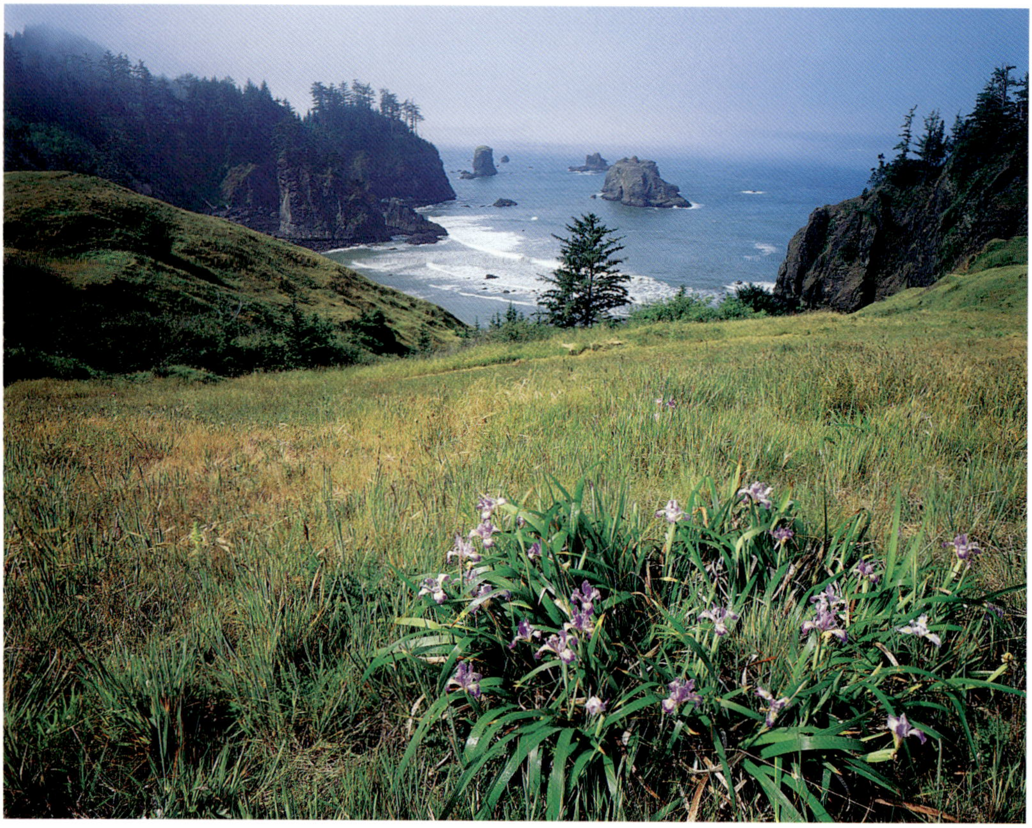

Wild iris bloom on grassy hillside overlooking offshore sea stacks at Boardman State Park *(Southern Coast)* STEVE TERRILL

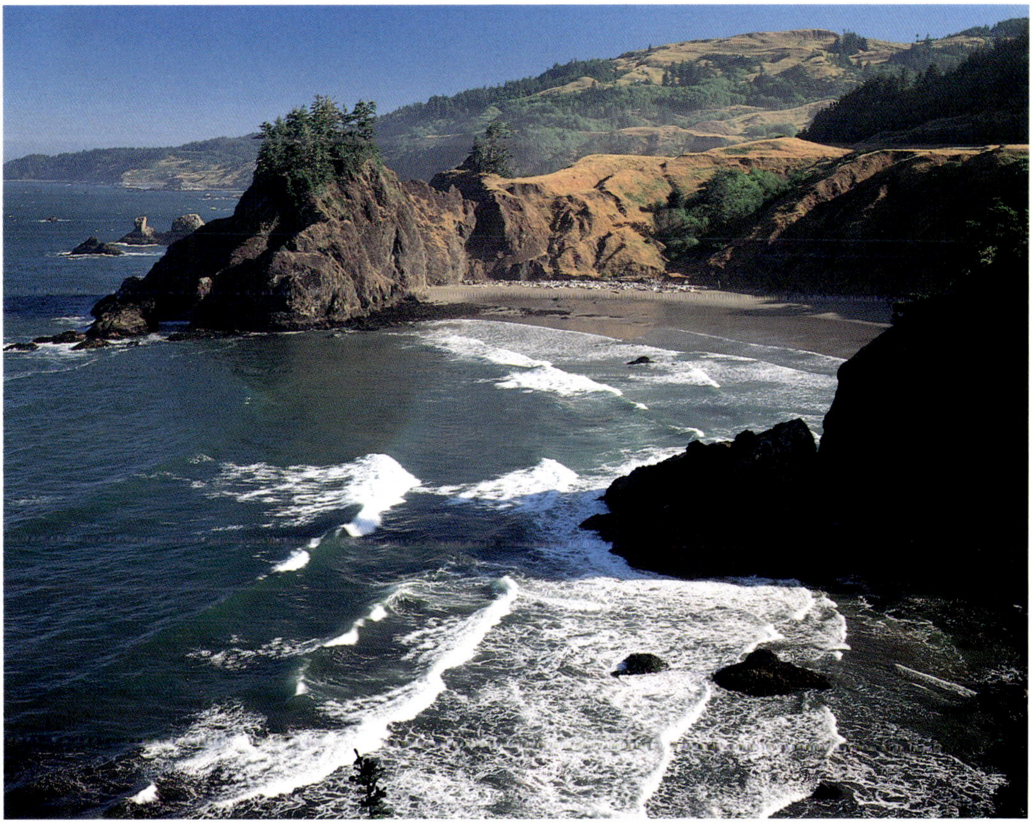

Afternoon light on one of the many headlands that reach into the Pacific, at Boardman State Park *(Southern Coast)* STEVE TERRILL

This park is named after Samuel H. Boardman, who in 1929 became Oregon's first state park superintendent. For the next twenty-one years, he had the vision to protect many areas of the Oregon coast for the public's enjoyment and richly earned the title of "Father of Oregon State Parks."